Thirty-Three Years in the Trenches

Memoirs of a Sussex Working Man

PETER RICHARDS

Thirty-Three Years in the Trenches

Memoirs of a Sussex Working Man

**An oral autobiography
compiled by
NICK OSMOND**

*With contributions from Dan Horgan, Tony Bennett
and Mark, Stefan, Stewart and Wendy Richards*

Published by

White Cockade Publishing
71 Lonsdale Road
Oxford OX2 7ES

Tel. 01865 510411
mail@whitecockade.co.uk
www.whitecockade.co.uk

500 592698

The publisher and authors are most grateful to the Lipman-Miliband Trust
and the Barry Amiel & Norman Melburn Trust for their contributions
towards production costs.

British Library Cataloguing-in-Publication Data

A catalogue record for this book is available from the British Library.

ISBN 1 873487 10 X paperback

Illustrations

Front cover: Peter Richards, 1990s.
Back cover: Peter and Nick in conversation, 1998.
Opposite title page: 1. Peter Richards, 1991.

We dedicate this book to all the men who made Peter's thirty-three years in the trenches endurable by their stoicism and sense of humour in harsh uncomfortable conditions

ILLUSTRATION ACKNOWLEDGEMENTS

We thank all who have helped in providing illustrations and giving permission to reproduce them. All photographs other than those listed below were taken by Peter Richards.

Family snaps 2, 3; Sara Ferrand 24; Haslemere Educational Museum 7; Mike Pearson 6; Mark Richards back cover, 16; Stewart Richards front cover, 1, 17, 20, 23; Wendy Richards 12; Royal London Society for the Blind 4; Alan Tate 14; unknown photographers 10, 13, 18; F. Witten & J. Hoare 5.

CONTENTS

Part Two: Life in the Trenches

Part Three: As Others See Us

FOREWORD

The trenches are the ones we come across almost every day in our streets: red and white boards barring the way, pavements dug up, dust and din, weatherbeaten men in helmets and scruffy clothes who seem to belong to a different world from inconvenienced pedestrians like us.

One of these men was Peter Richards, who for thirty-three years was a ganger in charge of a team laying gas mains in the Brighton and South London areas. He wasn't fighting a war, but life in the trenches was always a struggle and sometimes a battle. He is one of the millions who are excluded from mainstream biography and hidden from history because they are supposed to be 'just ordinary people'. Yet it is by the intelligent labour of these people that we have progressed from smoky hovels to the unconsidered comfort of central heating and modern kitchens.

Peter isn't 'just ordinary'. He is a complex individual whose darker side is balanced by the humour, the wit and the way with words which go with a quickfire intelligence. On a good day the conversation crackles. He's highly conscious, kind, amusing and original, a gifted mimic, a racy raconteur and a good friend. The feeling for what he's talking about is always there, in the voice and the body-language as well as the words. He's got many talents. In different circumstances he might have become the skipper of a fishing boat, or a photographer, or an absent-minded professor. As things turned out, his life took him into the trenches.

The book is the product of cooperation: Peter's oral autobiography as told to me in recorded conversations which took place between 1998 and the year 2000, mainly with Peter himself but also with his close friends, his wife and his three sons. The transcript of the recordings, together with some extra written contributions, was edited down to make an unpublished 'Family Edition' of the book which comes out at about 220,000 words.

We did not necessarily record Peter's exierences in the order they happened, and he does not recall his life as a continuous history with long-term themes and perspectives. It comes out as a series of self-contained episodes, stories he tells about his past. They make sense of that past, but they are not joined up, and there are intriguing spaces between them.

In consultation with Peter and our very clear-sighted publisher, Perilla Kinchin, I have brought the 'Family Edition' down to about a third of its original length by further selection, ordering and editing. So the book is also a biography, reflecting my sense of who Peter is and what I see as the periods, patterns and meanings of his life.

He and the other contributors were not speaking into thin air. Unlike the traditionally invisible ghost-writer who has to pretend to be the subject, I am present throughout the book as the person who is spoken to, and I hope you readers will be able to feel as you turn the pages that you have slipped into my shoes and that Peter and then Dan and Tony, Wendy, Mark, Stewart and Stefan, are talking directly to you.

Peter and the others are the subjects and not the objects of their history. They contributed willingly to what they saw as a positive enterprise; they decided what to talk about and, as importantly, what not to talk about. I may have elicited and recorded the words, but the words are theirs and they are speaking for themselves. Even on the printed page the rhythm and texture of each voice can still be heard.

Parts One and Two tell the story of Peter as he sees himself. Part Three is Peter as he is seen by the people who know him well enough to fill in some of the spaces between his stories.

The punctuation sometimes favours speech patterns over standard grammar. One or two names have been changed. A few of the written passages are included where contributors were making a particularly detailed or important statement.

Finally, Peter and I would like to thank friends and family for their generous support and encouragement.

Nick Osmond
Brighton, March 2001

Part One:
Growing

GROWING PAINS

Only child   I was an only child, and my parents separated before I was five. I was born on 23 October 1938, in Cricklewood.

I can remember very little of the early years, or of my father, and I've had no contact with him. I think his family was Spanish, perhaps the name was changed from Ricardos. He may have left my mother for another woman. She told me he was a dance-hall Johnny but never said much about him. She's never bad-mouthed him, only inasmuch that he never sent anything for my keep. On my birth certificate it's got his occupation at the time, lathe operator.

Eye thing   I never had any sight in my left eye. When I was born it was sort of milky and cloudy. I was a breech delivery and I've been told the damage may have been caused by forceps.

As a kid I really wasn't much aware of that eye. I was aware that my eyes weren't very good because I had to wear those bloody awful dark glasses with leather bits on the side from as long back as I can remember. And I was always embarrassed by them. I wasn't allowed to take them off at all.

I can't remember exactly at what age I ceased to wear them but by the time I went to Secondary Modern school, I was wearing normal glasses and that was when I was made aware of the eye itself and how different it looked. It was always being commented upon by the kids, you know what kids are like, they're very cruel. I mean, Nelson, and One-eye, and Whelk, Isaiah, and all this sort of thing. Whether I closed it subconsciously so that people couldn't see it I don't know.

And funnily enough when I moved to another school, I remember the teacher very well, a man called Mr Tattin, who was very kind, but at the same time he embarrassed me by always making me sit near the front, always asking me if I could see. I mean he was doing it with the best will in the world but I wished to God he hadn't. I preferred to sit in the back with the smart-arses, which I did subsequently. Because I didn't have any problems seeing the board.

2. Peter at about five with his father: the only record he has of him.

My right eye is OK, touch wood. I don't think it has changed a lot, but when I was about twelve, thirteen, they diagnosed glaucoma, which means you're subject to cataracts that can set in early.

Round about that time they decided for cosmetic reasons they would remove the discoloured left eye and give me a prosthesis, which would draw less attention to my eye. It was made of plastic, as opposed to glass and it somehow fitted with the muscles at the back of the eye, that move the eye from side to side, up or down. Which is quite good and quite clever. But the eye still remained semi-closed a lot of the time. Again I think this was because I'd got used to it. And people used to think I just had what's called a lazy eye.

I go now and again to the Sussex Artificial Limb Centre – believe it or not – to get the eye polished, because especially when I was working it used to get gritty, and very sore, and I'd get a discharge from it. The woman there said she could make it so it stayed open more. But I thought I preferred it to do the closed thing, rather than have one of these staring eyes which a lot of people with artificial eyes have.

It's made me quite aggressive. Inasmuch that people made remarks. And the usual one was, if you don't shut up I'll close your other eye. Which was like a red rag to a bull to me, that really switched me on.

People think I consciously try and compensate for it. I don't know if I do but I'm always aware that I don't have as much sight as I would like. Which seems a bit ridiculous seeing that I've only ever had one eye and this amount of sight. But I've always been aware that maybe I can't see as much as other people. I always want to see more than I can see.

Yet some people are amazed at what I can see and how quick. I beam in on something and really that eye works hard. I mean when we were working at night on these gas installations, the next day I was absolutely washed out because of really concentrating very very hard.

Foster mothers   My mother Molly was a very attractive woman, she worked as a milliner before the war. Her best friend was May Cunningham, and for a time they lived together in Lansdowne Grove, Neasden, near a large marshalling yard. It was heavily bombed one Sunday afternoon and I remember sleeping in an air-raid shelter. The sound of sirens still makes the hairs go up on the back of my neck.

During the war my mother was drafted into the production of

15

Ascot water-heaters to release other women for war work. She met my stepfather Fred in the factory. I think they lived together but couldn't marry for some time because they had to wait for the divorce papers. Every day Fred would go to Somerset House to see if the documents had come through. When they did, it stated there was one child of the marriage who was dead, presumed killed in the blitz. But I exist and I've got my birth certificate to prove it.

3. Peter with 'Aunty May', at Landsowne Grove, Neasden, about 1943.

My first two schools were mainstream: Infants School in Villiers Road, in Willesden, a corrugated, green-painted, tin place, then a massive, frightening place off Western Avenue, Neasden. Next I was sent to a day-school for handicapped children. I can't for the life of me understand why unless it was because the kids were of mixed disabilities, some very obvious, like mental handicap and serious physical problems. Some of them wore callipers. I was picked up and taken to the school on a special bus and this I clearly remember as being very embarrassing. I never consider myself handicapped even though I had to wear those hideous dark glasses.

As my mother was working I spent a lot of time being looked after by relatives or family friends, who I think of as foster mothers. In Villiers Road there was Mrs Boddymead. When I revisited her house in the sixties, I was able to walk straight to the door even though I couldn't remember the number, but she'd died. When I was at the Western Avenue school I was cared for by May, then it was May's mother, Mrs Mack. May's daughter Josie protected me like a tigress with her young. After Mrs Mack, I was sleeping at Mrs Palmer's, a Welsh lady who lived under the Cunninghams. There was also Gladys, at Stonebridge Park, which didn't last long.

Blind school   When I was about six I was sent to a special boarding school for blind and partially sighted children. It was called Dorton House, a Jacobean manor in Buckinghamshire. I stayed there till I was eleven.

On the first day I went with my mother to Paddington Station where all the rest of the kids were saying goodbye to their parents. I didn't cry, I know I didn't. My strongest memory is the steam engine, I mean every boy had seen pictures of engines in books or whatever but I'd never been that close to a big steam engine before. To me it was a living, breathing beast that seemed full of energy impatient to be released. And the smell of it – if I smell hot oil and coal smoke now, that takes me straight back to Paddington Station in 1944.

Quite a few of the kids were crying, there was about six or seven of them in our compartment, I think mostly blind. The train pulled out through the grey London suburbs – everything seemed grey at that time – then we were into the green countryside.

At High Wycombe we all got off and changed trains to a much more humble country train going out on the branch line to Dorton Halt. We then walked through these very winding lanes, about a hundred or so kids hand in hand, and up to Dorton House. I don't think there was one car passed us.

Separation   We, the very young kids, were segregated virtually straight away, we went to a room which was separate from the bigger children. I remember having to go to bed at half-past five. Then when the lights went out at seven-thirty, first of all it was very quiet and then you could gradually hear snuffling, then kids sobbing. There was quite a lot of that.

And then one particular couple that I did think was very sad, it was a pair of twins, Alec and Teresa. Who were totally blind, and who were separated that first night. In the morning when they were re-united those two clung to each other like they were drowning. And they used to rock, in unison. Which quite a lot of blind kids did. I don't know why they rock but I've seen animals in captivity do it.

Tell!   The tradition was that someone in the dormitory would 'tell'. Someone would make up a story after lights went out, which was totally forbidden, and tell a story.

It wasn't grown men with whiskers and stuff, it was invariably boys in heroic situations. Never handicapped. Even if a blind guy was telling the story he wouldn't tell it as a blind person, he'd tell it as a person that had got all his faculties. One of the favourite stories was the adventures of a boy that had a horse, a dog and a gun. They were sort of essential ingredients. Now one person's job was to keep one ear very sharply tuned to the particular master that was on duty that evening, and warn everybody. Sometimes it worked, sometimes it didn't.

We had one particular master who would creep up very quietly so no one would hear him, and then he would jump through the dormitory door shouting, Out all those who were talking. And people would gradually own up, and he'd have them out and they would be slippered. And a plimsoll on a pyjama-clad bottom is pretty sore. There was one night when quite a few people were talking and this man, who had a terrible reputation, did try and slipper everybody in the dormitory, which was quite a feat. I didn't get it because the guy that was slippered before me was so frightened he peed himself while across the master's knee.

Dedicated   The other teachers there, I can truthfully say that I liked all of them, I had a great deal of affection and respect for most of them, and the domestic staff. They were very kind. Some of them seemed a bit strict but in hindsight I don't think they were too rigorous. And when you're in a classroom being taught by someone and you see the same person at mealtimes and first thing in the morning sort of thing, you do have a different relationship with them than you would a teacher that you only meet from nine until four. And I think these people were dedicated.

Hold your tongue!   The only people I didn't like, we occasionally got the person that had got God. It tended to be the sort of supervisor that looked after the kids in dormitories, or at mealtimes. I never felt comfortable in their presence, and they were usually the most rigorous in inflicting discipline. There was one particular woman, the very small kids were going for a walk through the woods, it wasn't even on the road. And we were walking and chattering and everything, and we were made to walk in silence and told to hold our tongues by this woman. I remember lots of us actually did get hold of our tongues and hold them.

4. *Children listening to a story under a yew tree at Dorton House School for the Blind in Buckinghamshire.*

Reading   When I went to a Secondary Modern school later I was very aware of how much more advanced, or sophisticated if you like, the way that English was taught at the boarding school was. From seven we were taught the structure of grammar, verbs, adverbs and all that sort of thing. And also a lot of literature, I'm talking about Greek mythology, for example, in particular. And the work of Dickens. Which is not heavy by anybody's standards,

19

but I didn't encounter that until maybe the fourth year in Secondary Modern school.

We had a library at the school, in Braille, and these are MASSIVE books, they're much bigger than A4 and from what I remember two inches thick. Very heavy, very big. And the pages were varnished so the upraised Braille wouldn't obviously wear down with constant use. So I was reading in Braille, but cheating by looking at the dots. I read books at home, I had books at a very early age. But I can't remember that point when I actually learned to read.

Music   Music was very very important. You could hear a piano being practised almost any time of the night or day. So-and-So would be excused lessons to go and do his half-hour practice. There was even a piano in one of the bathrooms.

And it was all classical music, there was no modern, pop or anything like that. In fact some of the older boys did start to form a jazz band and that was virtually underground for a term or so. I don't remember them saying, You can't have it, but it just didn't happen. And I did get a certain amount of taste for classical music which I'm glad that I got. I think the school was run a bit on public school lines. It was closer to a public school than it was Dr Barnado's, let's put it that way.

Outdoors   The kids were outside all the time. Except when Dick Barton was on the radio, the omnibus edition Saturday, there would only be one or two of us outside and I'd be one of the two. I was always outside.

The grounds were big, large areas of grass and many trees, ancient yews, very large pines, oaks and many others. Tree climbing was very popular with the boys and the blind boys could hold their own with the partially sighted. When the new matron first arrived at Dorton House she was horrified to see blind small boys, nonchalantly clambering from branch to branch at what to her seemed dizzying heights.

I think the last time I saw my father was at Dorton House, one Parents' Day. My mother and stepfather were there and he rolled up with a blond. I sensed the atmosphere. He and I were playing war-games, creeping through the jungle to shoot Japs, with a cap-rifle that Fred had made for me.

Holidays The first holidays from Dorton House were spent at Ealing with my mother's sister, Aunty Gwen, that would be Christmas 1944. After that my mother was living with May and I sometimes went there at weekends. During the week I would be spending the nights with another series of foster mothers, all different.

After a couple of years at Dorton House I moved in permanently with my mother and stepfather who had married and set up house together at Montpelier Avenue, Ealing. My foster parents would have me during the day. It was a solitary time.

I am sailing When I was about eight or nine, I had this little boat with a yellow sail, it was wooden with quite a deep keel, made of steel, and these yellow plastic sails. It was only about twelve inches long. The sails worked quite well and obviously being plastic, they didn't waste any wind at all, so it was quite a nice little boat. I spent hours and hours, well days and days, sailing this little yellow boat on Walpole Park Pond, in Ealing. I don't think I've ever played with anything as much since, or before, I was obsessed with it. I remember hostilely defending it when some smart-arsed kids from Walpole Grammar School, typical sort of grammar school kids at that time, were very contemptuous of this boat with a yellow sail. They said things like, Ah you never see a yacht with a yellow sail, and certainly not a plastic one, and were very dismissive. And I defended it by saying, Yes you do get boats in Egypt with yellow sails. I didn't know anything about Egypt or anything else, but it was almost like a personal attack on me. I really did love that boat.

It used to sail quite nicely and get stuck up in bits of the pond but then the wind eventually would change and the boat would come back. I never had it on a string. I imagined I was sailing in it to somewhere exotic, somewhere warm where there were dark people. So that was a very important part of my childhood.

My mother also took me for a trip down the Thames on a paddle steamer, the Royal Eagle, from Tower Bridge to Margate. I was totally fascinated, going down through the London Docks which were still very very busy. And then going down to the engine room and seeing all that steam, and the pistons and everything, oh it was fantastic. And I sort of hero-worshipped the matelots that used to throw the lines ashore and handle the ropes and all that sort of thing. I thought that was extreme.

I read all the usual boys' books, *Treasure Island, Coral Island*, but I never imagined that I'd have anything to do with the sea at all. I just thought I'd never get near a boat. When I got bigger I did use to go to Gunnersbury Park occasionally, and you could hire boats out, but I always scorned the paddle ones and preferred the rowing boats. They were proper boats.

Stepfather   During the summer holidays I can remember going with my mother and Fred down to the park and playing cricket with him, and him teaching me how to hold a bat straight and all the rest of it, and how to bowl. He used to make me things, like that cap-rifle, which he made quite a good job of. He was quite a good carpenter, his father was a cabinet-maker, as well as a master-builder. He made me a cricket bat. I used to buy those balsa wood aircraft kits by Kiel Kraft that were all the rage at the time, and I can remember him showing me how to make those. Also he taught me how to mend my own shoes. Which was an important skill I haven't used since.

After the war Fred was a school buildings inspector for the LCC, he was based at County Hall. I don't know if he's shaped me politically but he was always a Labour voter. *The Ragged Trousered Philanthropists* was his book, I did discuss it with him as I was reading it. And he did tell me, in the twenties or thirties when things were very very tight, him walking from place to place, as opposed to getting a bus, in case he walked past a place where he could have gone in and got a job. That's left quite a large impression on me.

And yet my parents were supporters of royalty as well. How can you be a socialist, or think socially, and support the very thing that's putting its foot on your neck? It's not just them, but they represent undeserved privilege, which I think is wrong and holds back the working-class population who don't have the initial kick-start in education such as prep school and the finance to support a student through university. If you've got a hallmark you don't have to shine.

Not my father   It's very hard to think of Fred in a positive sense. Yes, he did clothe and feed me until I was fifteen. And he did play actually in a dance band at one time, I think in the early forties, saxophone and clarinet. But I'd always been aware right from day one that he was not my father. I didn't initially regard him as an intruder, but he was somebody else. Not my father. Putting it crudely, I'm not of his blood, that's it. When I was feeling my resentment against him, the fact that he wasn't my own father made it stronger. I think I could have taken a lot more cuffs and stuff from my own father. I don't resent my father leaving, I resent Fred coming on the scene if you like.

He did make me know what I didn't want to be like. I didn't want to be like him under any circumstances. Not being pink and fat, they're the very obvious things. But also just the way everything had to be approached very carefully, he would never put one foot in front of the other unless he'd thought about it carefully. Nothing would be done irrationally, nothing would be spontaneous. Whenever you would come in wild with enthusiasm about something or other he would put the damper on it, Fred would put the dampers on virtually everything. He never did anything to excess, he worked steadily, he saved, he never had a car till well after I left home.

I think kids like adults, now and again, to show they are human. I never got the impression that Fred was human. I just think I found him boring.

New boy   When I was eleven, that would be 1949, I was taken to a psychologist to see if I could handle a Secondary Modern school. The answer was yes. He said I was bright, but not brilliant. I was sent to Drayton Green School, West Ealing. I was the only new boy, and not only that, I didn't know any of the other boys. The first day, that was particularly traumatic.

The form master, a Mr Stern, told us to draw a two-inch margin all the way through our exercise books. So I got a ruler but instead of doing a margin I started doing two-inch-spaced lines right across the page. He held the book up to the class and he said, Look what this stupid boy's done. And I was very very embarrassed because everyone dutifully shrieked with laughter. I never forgave him for that. I'd never had any formal teaching of writing. I thought then and I think now that was an extremely insensitive and stupid thing to do.

And then, he'd left the room for some reason or other, the kids all started to ask me where I'd come from, what school I went to. And I was very loath to say that I'd been to a blind school. I don't know why I should feel that, but a lot of the time and even today I won't say I went to a blind school. I said, Oh I went to Dorton House and it was a boarding school and that's it.

Fight   And then the inevitable question, Can you fight? Yeah, I can fight. Can you fight him? Yeah. Can you fight him? Yeah. Would you fight him? Yeah. And they eventually got round to this bespectacled kiddy, his name was Tony Day, quite a scruffy kid at the back of the class, Would you fight him? Yeah. Would you fight him at playtime? Yeah. I thought, God, what am I getting into?

So playtime came and the kids had formed like a circle round and started baying for blood. And then we set to and this guy just lammed into me, I don't know if I landed any punches at all, there was lots of blood and I think it was all mine. Unless his knuckles were bleeding of course. And next thing it's been broken up by a couple of masters and we were marched up to the headmaster's study, a Mr Leigh-Smith, who I think was a very kind man, and we were given a severe ticking off and dismissed. After this Tony Day and I, the classic boy's story, were the best of mates. And that was it.

At school it smoothed my passage. I was labelled as someone who had the bottle and I didn't get picked on at all. But my mother was absolutely livid with me, because my face was all marked up and I'd got cut knees. There was no sympathy whatsoever, and I thought at the time, I don't want you to mother and smother me, but, well, come on. But in a way I suppose I'm glad I established my own role at school.

Latch-key kid   I became a latch-key kid, arriving home before my parents. I drew great strength and solace from knowing there was a period before my mother and stepfather came home when I could have sobbed my heart out if I'd wanted to, though I never did.

Ironically, I took my eleven-plus after I'd got to Drayton Green. And failed. I stayed less than a year. Then my mother and step-father moved to Rayners Lane, a boring Nash suburb, suburbia at its worst. This meant moving to another Secondary Modern, Roxeth Manor in Eastcote Lane. This time the first day was OK and the school was as different from Drayton Green as chalk and cheese. I was in the A-stream class and it wasn't too bad. My English was good, my arithmetic bad.

Pillow stains   One morning my mother had gone to work and my stepfather had called me downstairs and I was in my pyjamas. And he's got a pillowcase there and he said, What are these stains on the pillow? I said, Well I don't know, dunno, no idea. So he wouldn't let it go, he said, Well what have you been up to? I said, I haven't been up to anything. So he said, You been playing with yourself? I said, No.

And he said, Right, drop your pyjama trousers. I thought, What the hell's going on? So I dropped them. He stared at my genitals for what seemed ages, he said, Right pull your trousers up. Don't fiddle with yourself, he said, and I'm not satisfied with your explanation about those stains. I said, Well I just don't know what they are. And it's possible that, some people, you salivate when you're asleep. Or I used to get quite a lot of discharge from one of my eyes.

I didn't understand at first what he was getting at, then when it did dawn I laughed, the vision of myself using my pillow as a sort of surrogate female I thought was hilarious. But at the same time I really didn't like the way he was handling it, or treating me.

I like other teenagers did dabble in onanism, but I never left anything for anybody else to clear up. Always there were tissues, always privacy. And I also knew it was a natural thing to do. I don't know why I knew, but at boarding school older boys tell you that it's something everybody does. And I first got the sensation, I always remember it, climbing a rope in the gym. Quite a few boys had experienced the same thing, that was the first time that you'd had an erection or ejaculated. When you're climbing a rope obviously, the way it goes between your legs and rubs against you.

Anyway I don't know if it was a week later, I was laying in bed and I had my hands behind my head. I was thinking about something or the other, not sex, that's for sure. And I heard the bottom stair creak, and I knew that someone was coming up the stairs and I thought, why are they being so quiet, it's not that late, and then the bedroom door burst open and and my stepfather jumped into the room and punched me straight in the balls. Not a word was spoken. And then he just went out.

Hate   And that really did make me really hate him, really, the bastard. And I also tied my mother in with that, because she used to do the washing, so she must have drawn his attention to it. I never forgave them both for that.

I thought I would definitely do something drastic to him. I even contemplated killing him, because he was getting inside my head. And initially I thought of knifing him, I thought, No that's no good because he'd possibly take it off me, I would do it with something heavy like a hammer, from behind.

I even worked out what penalty I'd get. I knew they couldn't hang me but I thought I would go to Borstal. For how many years I didn't know. But I naïvely came to the conclusion that as I had been to boarding school I would be able to survive Borstal. I thought about it quite cold-bloodedly. But because I tend not to make decisions and react quickly, the idea gradually faded and the prospect of me leaving home was on the horizon anyway.

I suppose if it hadn't been for this pillow stains thing, I would possibly be saying now, Oh well, Fred's not where I'm at, nothing like me, but he did the best as he saw it at the time. Age would have taken the corners off.

Out   I was always out. I'd go without a meal so that I could stay out, and not go home. They were always trying to censor the sort of people I knocked about with, although they didn't get to know any of them properly, because none of them were ever allowed to come in. When they called for me they had to wait on the doorstep. I can remember two boys actually allowed inside the house. One was a guy called Robin Lesley at South Harrow, he sat next to me in class. When I'd had the plastic eye put in he came round with some comics and sweets which the class had had a whip-round and bought for me.

Even kids that lived a few doors up the road, whose parents my parents used to chat to, they weren't allowed in either. And I used to feel bad about this. I could go in any of my friends' houses, I was always invited in just to wait five minutes or whatever, but anybody that called for me, couldn't. And that's embarrassing, especially when you're about fifteen.

There was lots of trouble about me being out late. What's considered late now would have been out of the question.

When I was fourteen I joined the ATC, the Air Training Corps, and we cadets had concessionary tickets to this special ice-rink at Wembley, about six or seven of us. The rail ticket, everything, was booked as a party. And because we didn't leave until about half past ten at night, I didn't get home till about midnight.

My mother was going absolutely mad and my stepfather got really nasty. I always remember the only words he kept repeating, You're not worth two penn'orth of fucking cold piss. Over and over again, in spite of me saying, I couldn't come away because we were in a party, check up, ask the man, go and see the officer next week, I couldn't leave any earlier. I got a smack in the mouth, I remember that quite clearly. And that's what it was like.

I wasn't defiant, though. I thought, well I can understand you being worried, which I've been with my kids when they've been out late. But to go on like this, and totally ignore the reasons and the justification, is ridiculous. I knew that at the time.

Coffee bars We used to hang around the streets mostly, because on this vast Nash's estate there was nothing. We used to go to Rayners Lane to hang around the tube station and a coffee bar called The Gum Tree. They played very good music, good modern jazz, which I was into anyway. It was just at the advent of coffee bars. There'd been milk bars, that sort of chromium fifties thing, but these were absolutely new. They were open late, they had espresso with a machine.

They were considered to be real dens of iniquity, which was ridiculous. Various people wore berets and dark glasses to try and look like the sort of arty types you used to get in France, the left bank or whatever. We used to talk, nearly all the time. We would argue about politics, about morals, about sex or whatever, that's what we did.

We also frequented Rudy's Café, but that was a more down-to-earth establishment and Rudy every now and then would say, Give the seats an airing, boys. Because we'd been there for bloody hours. There was nowhere else to go. We couldn't go to the pubs. There were youth clubs, but the crowd that I knocked around with didn't like them, didn't like the idea of sanctimonious vicars doing their bit and all that went with that. Youth clubs didn't hit the spot.

Mock bundles Another thing we used to do was what we called mock bundles. We would do anything to provoke a situation, one of us would be the victim, and the other three or four would be the people who were going to run up and jump on this guy and

27

knock him down and beat him senseless. We often used to do this in a fairly crowded place, so everyone would be thinking, Christ, what's going on. We never did it for real, but it looked convincing, if it was dark. And one night my stepfather and my mother were going somewhere and they came across us doing this, and they thought it was real. Oh, Jesus Christ. Frog-marched me onto the bus, oh there was hell to pay. He didn't hit me over that. But I said, It's just a laugh. And then one of my mates didn't help matters by coming up to the bus before it pulled away and said, in the north-west London vernacular of the time, It's just a bit of 'ank mister. The guy didn't speak like this normally, but that confirmed I was mixing with a load of hooligans.

Everything I seemed to do was wrong. My mother told me from the age of ten onwards, constantly, that I was the biggest disappointment of her life. And you get a bit fed up with that, after a bit. They wanted me to be more respectable, yes, they didn't like any of that street business at all, they were frightened of it. And I think my mother was very frightened of me getting involved heavily with a girl of any sort. She was saying, Always knock around in a crowd, don't split up into twos, always go with a crowd. God knows, I'd done my carnal experiments years before at Dorton House, before I was eleven. Although we were kept separate, there were ways of meeting girls. There was bits where there wasn't a fence, you could have assignations. I knew what was what.

Burnt When I was thirteen or fourteen I got infatuated with some girl round the back of where we lived, and I wrote her a note saying 'I love you, Daphne.' The next thing I know is she has shown it to all her friends and Christ, I can never remember feeling so mortified as that, and I thought, I'm never, ever, going to do that again. I mean that hurt. An absolute rejection, it was awful. I handled it inasmuch that I didn't take it out on anybody, and I didn't get suicidal or anything as desperate as that, but it's like getting burnt, every time you get burnt you're that much more cautious the next time. But I think that's common to a lot of teenagers.

On the road I never had a new bike. I suppose I might have got one if I'd passed the eleven-plus or something. But on my thirteenth birthday, I think it was, with my birthday card was the key to the lock on my stepfather's bike. Which meant I got his bike, I suppose you'd call it a tourer. But it did open up quite a few areas to me that I hadn't previously been in. I could roam further away. And of course I could do a paper round which earned me I think fifteen shillings a week pocket money, which was handy. It had a three-speed, it wasn't all that special but it did get me around, and also where I'd been left out of things with other friends from school or whatever, I could now join in and go places with them.

And one of the first places that I remember going to on that bike, we cycled out to Windsor and Runnymede, from Rayners Lane, this horrible Nash's estate. It was in the summer, or late spring.

I was stopped by this burly policeman in Windsor itself, who demanded that I put my shirt back on. And I said, Why? He said, Because you're not allowed to ride through Windsor without a shirt. I said, It's a free country. No, it's not, he said, it's a bye-law, you are not allowed to be in Windsor without a shirt, put your shirt on or you'll be nicked. I was only thirteen or fourteen, so obviously I had to put my shirt on. Another time, I had the distinction of being told to bugger off by one of the Coldstream Guards at Windsor Castle when I was poking round somewhere I shouldn't.

Black man   The next thing was that we were by the river, and it was my first encounter with a black man. They were still very much a curiosity. Where I lived I'd not seen any black men other than a few American airforce black guys, not many of those. I'm pretty sure these were Jamaicans, they were painting up the pleasure boats that were going to be on the Thames. And this bloke, who seemed immense to me, I don't know if he was seven foot, in a loud voice, with his Jamaican accent, he said, Would you like a cream, boy? I didn't understand what he meant but I thought I'd say yes just in case. And what he meant was ice-cream, and if I went and got them he'd buy me one. Which I did, and that's my first experience of a black man. And he was nice. I mean, why shouldn't he be?

Private property   And then the next experience was, we went swimming at Runnymede and swam across to Runnymede Island. And was then confronted by this bloody great boxer dog that started snarling, this that and the other, and this guy, about the same age as us, told us it was private property and we were trespassing, and we had to swim back. I didn't get very snotty, I just said, Yeah all right, we'll swim back but let's catch our breath, because there's quite a current there and you've got to be a bit careful. Anyway he got chatting and I think his name was Hipwell, and his uncle was Sir Walter Palm of Palm Toffees, it turned out. And we got quite pally with this youngster – well the same age as us – and he invited us into the house, and I actually remember sitting with my wet bum, in my swimming trunks, on top of the table that the Magna Carta was allegedly signed on. His father, who was I think Hipwell of Hipwell Breweries, I'd never heard of them before or since, collected horse brasses, and one room was completely covered, walls and ceiling, with horse brasses. And we got quite friendly with this guy and paid a few visits there. That was quite nice, and that was through cycling out there, that was good. We didn't take the ferry, no, we'd swim across.

I had a girlfriend at that time and we used to cycle out to a place called Ruislip Lido, which was a fenced-off area with quite a large lake, where there were pleasure boats and woods and things, and I used to go over to the Common, which was adjacent to this place, with this girlfriend of mine. We'd do quite innocent sort of snogging and stuff on the Common. Later she committed suicide, not over me I might add. Which was very sad because she was a very nice girl. But she got God and I couldn't handle that. She became a Covenanter, I think they were called. But having girlfriends round at home, that was just out of the question.

Constriction   I do know from my peer group that my childhood and schooldays were far more restrictive than theirs were. I didn't want to be at home, I didn't want to be there at all. I'd been away from home, I'd experienced other forms of existence, I knew how other people lived. The umbilical cord had been cut an awful long time and I didn't have any of those feelings that one should have for one's mother. I just didn't have them and that was it. My mother and stepfather put the brake on, or shot down, everything I stood for or thought or felt. From the clothes that I wanted to wear, to the company that I wanted to keep, everything.

FARMER'S BOY

Into the sticks   I was fifteen and approaching school-leaving time. I decided that whatever job I did, the way things were with my stepfather and my mother, I had to get away from home. I thought maybe the merchant navy but they wouldn't wear this at all, they said they wouldn't sign any papers or anything. I then toyed with the idea of the Forces but the reality of the eye problem drove me to think, That's not possible either. I knew I couldn't stand working indoors, as I found it more and more irksome to be indoors at school all the time. So the only alternative was working on a farm. I mentioned this at school to a careers teacher, and there was this post-war scheme sponsored by the YMCA called British Boys for British Farms. British boys for British farmers, more like.

I'd no experience whatsoever but I'd had the rural thing at my boarding school in the depths of Buckinghamshire. I spent nearly all my time outdoors and we went to do farm visits. It became almost a part of everyday life, seeing cows and cow-muck, and always the fear when we were going on walks, Has this field got a bull in it?

So I applied to join this scheme, got an acceptance letter and the date to go and attend this training place, which was one of several in the country. This particular one was in North Cadbury in Somerset, near Frome. It was based in Cadbury Court which was a stately home. It was partly occupied by Lady Cadbury, I seem to remember.

Anyway I left school on the Friday and caught the train on the Monday, the date was 8 March 1954. I didn't know any of the other boys. They were quite a mixed crew, some dressed in the height of Teddy boy fashion of the time, which I thought was a bit incongruous for going into the sticks. Nevertheless. We were met at the station, taken to this house and given a briefing by the warden. He was a short man, quite heavy, who I would say nowadays had all the complexes of a short man, very aggressive and very full of himself. His wife worked there too as a sort of housekeeper and he had a young son.

He asked for volunteers. The first week you worked either as a kitchen orderly, or a sort of domestic inside the main building. This was one way they made it more economical. So I elected to go to the kitchen. It would mean getting up early but at least it wouldn't be all day. So I thought.

Kitchen boy   We were woken up about half-past five to go and prepare the breakfast for the boys working out on the farms. And this was OK because there was a proper cook there, telling you what to do. But it was a bit of a panic to get all the breakfasts ready by I think six-thirty. And after that there was the clearing up in the kitchen and we had our breakfast.

Then it was start to prepare the vegetables for the evening meal. My particular job was to do the spuds. There was an electric potato machine. The theory was you dug out the eyes first, but I put the spuds straight in the machine. I found that if you left them in there long enough, it took enough skin and potato off so it got down beyond the eyes. Mind you all the spuds were spherical, and my week on duty the spud consumption went up by fifty per cent. But that's what I did.

Something happened my second night. We had to prepare supper, quite late. It was cocoa and a lump of bread and jam or something like that, a bit prison-like. Not speaking from experience. And because I didn't like cocoa I had a cup of milk. The guy working with me, who I think was an ex-Borstal boy, had some bread and jam. We thought nothing of it, but then after we'd cleared up, everybody had to attend prayers, this is about ten o'clock. And this warden said some prayers and waffled on about something or other, then after prayers he said, Right, dismiss, go to bed, except for you, Richards, and you – I can't remember the other boy's name. We thought, What's this? He said, All right, get out the bumper. This is a thing for polishing big floors. Right, you polish the main floor. I said, What for, we're kitchen domestics, we've done our bit, we're not house domestics. He said, This is a punishment. I said, Punishment, what for? So he said, You had half a cup of milk, Richards, and you, So-and-So, had some bread and jam, you stole it. I couldn't believe it. I said, What do you mean, stole it? I don't like cocoa so I had some milk, it was in the kitchen, what's wrong with that? He said, You had something you weren't supposed to have. So I thought, Well I'm here, it's the second day,

I don't want to go home, so I'm not going to make waves.

That set the pattern. And every night a boy had to say a prayer, it's part of the participation thing, and I'd shuffled to the back of the queue every time. I didn't want to say any bloody prayer, I didn't believe in any of that nonsense. But when I finally couldn't escape any more, my prayer went something along these lines: Please God make us patient with those in authority that oppress us, and God knows what, and the warden kept on saying, Amen, Amen, Amen and eventually I did shut up. But it didn't do me any good.

Learning by doing   After the week as a domestic I went to work every day on this farm, training. I was still living at Cadbury Court. Training was a misnomer. I thought it would consist of lectures, and standing and watching, observing, but it wasn't that at all. Depending on your reliability, which the farmer could assess pretty quickly, you actually worked, as a farm boy. My job was to assist the cowman, clean the chicken battery out, help clean the pigs out, and any other work that came along. And once it was established that I could do these things that's what I did every day. At least I got a variety of jobs, whereas some boys on their training farms might have just one thing to do and that was all they did. One particular London boy moved a heap of manure in a wheelbarrow, tons of it, day in day out.

My farmer was Mr Baber. And his wife was a nice woman, she used to give me a lump of cake and a cup of coffee, ten o'clock, and he also gave me half a crown a week, which he wasn't obliged to do. And he was kind. We did have lectures sometimes in the evening, but most of us were so knackered, because we were doing hard physical work and long hours, that we weren't interested, we wanted to go to bed. And for fifteen- and sixteen-year-old boys to want to go to bed at ten o'clock must tell you how tired we were.

There was another thing with that training business. You would be taken in a shooting brake round to the various farms that were having the training boys, and you were made to get out and line up and the farmer would pick you, like he'd pick out a big horse or a strong bullock or something. Which I didn't like very much at all, but again I didn't want to make waves.

But I didn't fall out with the warden. I think he and I avoided each other as much as possible. I didn't like the man, and I think the place could have been a lot better run, quite frankly, but there you go.

Cowpuncher   After eight or ten weeks I was taken away to my farm where I would work, in Somerset. It was not even a hamlet, just a farm. Wellington was the nearest town of any size. The farmer was called Mr Betts, a very powerful man in his thirties with two or three kids and a big wife. And from day one he constantly reminded me that I was a Londoner. Was I a wide-boy or a spiv? If so he'd get me a wide tie and a trilby hat. It got to be a bit boring after a while. So he and I didn't get on. He was a brute, physically there was no way I could ever challenge a man like that. He could actually fell a cow, I've seen him put a cow on her knees with his fist, punching her, he was something else.

I had to share not only a bedroom but a bed with Mr Betts's nine-year-old son, which I didn't like at all. I'd been to boarding school and fostered, but I'd never shared a bed with anybody. Our bed was against the wall and I would sometimes hear Mr Betts in the next-door bedroom making romantic overtures to his wife. She'd be saying, Not tonoight moy dear, and his reply, in his growling Somerset brogue, would invariably be, You godoo 'ave 'er, you godoo 'ave 'er. I felt they were only one step up from the farmyard. Then we'd hear the headboard banging against the wall and the boy would ask, What are they doing? Having a cuddle, was the best I could come up with. That was the first time I'd overheard a couple making love.

River bathing   Again I was quite busy. My first Sunday the job was, get up early, help with the milking, take the eight cows two or three miles up this lane to a field called the Glebe Ground, which means it was ground that he'd rented off the Church, and pump with an old-style village pump enough water for the cows, and that's a hell of a lot of water to pump, because cows drink an awful lot of water, especially if they're in full milk, which these were. Then I had to go across another field or two, check the fences round this field and count the sheep.

But the dog didn't know what to do with the sheep, he just kept pushing them from one end of the field to the other, and they were panicking. Eventually one of the ewes, which had its full fleece on, went into this river. I had to get in as well and I'm trying to get this sheep back onto the bank, which took an awful lot of effort because although the river only came halfway up my thighs it was quite a fast current. But the trouble was the dog was running up and down the bank barking like crazy, which meant the sheep wouldn't even try to get out. So in the end I've got this ewe between my legs holding it with one hand, I've had to take my belt off with the other, and slash at the dog with the buckle end of my belt to drive him away. Eventually I did get her out of the river, and went back to the farm.

By this time it was getting quite late, I think it must have been about nine o'clock. I was wet from the river and from the fact that it was peeing down with rain. So I had my breakfast, went upstairs, changed into my casual gear, the only gear I had, and sat down in the other room. The next thing, the farmer's come storming in, he says, What do you think you're doing boy? I said, Well I've taken the cows up, counted the sheep, done everything you told me to, and that's it. He said, Your day's not finished till the milking shed's cleaned up. So then I timorously enquired as to whether he was paying me overtime. He said, I'm not paying you overtime, I've never paid a boy overtime yet and I'm not starting with you. And what's more, when you're sixteen, I'll get rid of you because your money goes up a pound a week. I remember those words as clear as anything and I think that's when I started to think politically.

Church parade   I was under contract to work for this guy for a year, and part of the contract was that I would go to church on Sundays. Obviously with the YMCA that was part of the deal. Which I didn't like, I thought, Oh Christ. The first Sunday as we came out of the church I was introduced to the Vicar and as I walked away he called the farmer back. Just before lunch the farmer took me aside, he said, By the way the Vicar was glad to see you attending church, but in future, can you dress a little more soberly? My dress was what was fashionable for teenagers at the time: square-tailed shirt worn outside jeans, jeans rolled up to half-way up the calf exposing yellow or white socks and crepe-soled shoes. This is what I wore. So I said, Well that's all I've got, I haven't got a suit, if he doesn't like it then that's it. So he said, Well that's all right then, you'd better not go to church. So I went, That's OK.

When there was nothing particular going on on the farm, like haymaking, he would put me in a ten-acre field with a slasher, to cut down thistles. This slasher was like a slightly curved sickle on the end of a long handle. I was given strict instructions that when I cut the thistles, not only was I to cut on the forward stroke, but then turn it over and cut on the backward stroke, thus giving the man double for what he was paying as it were. He was most emphatic about this: So you're not wasting any effort, every stroke is a cut. And you get quite proficient at this, but that was the most boring, lonely, soul-destroying job I think I've ever done because I'll swear they were growing back as quick as I cut them down, and I knew that this was only for him to give me something useful to do.

This guy milked by machine so all I was allowed to do was wash the muck off the cows' udders. I wasn't actually being taught things. You were shown something once and then expected to be able to do it.

And then going back to the farm in the evening, with just a couple of kids as company, and the farmer. There was no television then. A radio I think. And I used to go into Wellington, when I did have time off, to go and see the bright lights. But I didn't see many bright lights, because the bus brought me back to the farm too early.

Seeing stars Another incident was when one of his cows got a poisoned foot. Now in those days farmers didn't call out the vet unless they were absolutely desperate. So he was going to treat this poisoned foot himself. The treatment consisted of cutting the corner off a sack, stuffing this with boiling potatoes, I mean really hot, and then tying this round the cow's foot. Now this procedure involved putting a rope just above the foot, throwing a rope over a beam in the cowshed. He then hauled on the rope, lifting the cow's leg up, and my job was to put the poultice on this bloody foot. Well, I got the poultice on, and like any cloven-footed animal it's got a horn-like material, like your nails, on its foot, and initially it didn't feel the heat. And because she'd been quiet Mr Betts relaxed his grip on the rope, but before I could tie the baling-string round the sack to attach the poultice to her foot, the heat got to the cow through this tender spot where the septic bit was, and she lashed out. I clearly remember going head-over-heels backwards and smack up against the cowshed wall and actually seeing those lights whizzing round in front of me. And he just looked round and said, Come on boy, get up, don't mess about. And that was it. I was virtually stunned, but I still had to get back and put that bloody poultice on that foot.

Those are my fond memories of Mr Betts. I think I lasted a month. After that he got the YMCA to take me away. Said I wasn't suitable.

A kindly man   Then there was Mr Doggrel. He farmed in a place called Zeals, which is a hamlet adjacent to Stourhead in Wiltshire. Now he was a totally different farmer. Though again I would think quite a traditional man.

Stourhead is a well-known stately home and gardens. The first time I saw the place it was in the spring, we were approaching down this road, and I saw these pine trees going down the side of this hill, then this vast lake with what looked like Grecian temples but in fact were summer-houses, reflected in the water at the far end, and it was absolutely beautiful, a knockout. It really, literally, took my breath away.

And the farmer, he was a kindly man. I think he was tapping on a bit, because his eldest son was twenty-one so it would have made him about fifty-five, sixty, and to a fifteen-year-old that's tapping on. And I lodged with an elderly widow in what used to be a farmhouse down in a field, it didn't even have a path down to it. And this place was thatched. I can't remember the lady's name, but very kindly, very jolly. Mr Doggrel was a good farmer, he wouldn't let me do anything too heavy and his attitude to me was in complete contrast to Mr Betts.

I still had quite a lot of things to do and regular things like feeding the pigs and helping with the milking, again this was machine milking.

One incident there I can remember in a very kindly light. I was creosoting the inside of some chicken-houses and I got the stuff all over my face and became quite ill from this, and I was off for two days. But I remember quite clearly he paid me for those two days and was paying me over the rate, the minimum rate anyway, which for farmers is virtually unheard-of. This is through the YMCA again and theoretically I'm under a year's contract. They find me placements for a year, and I have to stay for a year wherever they place me.

Haymaking I remember one of the most pleasant jobs on this particular farm was haymaking. Now this was in the days before everything was mechanised, although 1954 isn't that long ago. The hay was cut in a spiral round the field and then it was left to lay there for a day. The next day, as long as it's dry, the job was to walk round the field turning the hay with pitchforks and there would be three or four of you. And this was really nice. It was not arduous, it didn't need all your concentration and you could talk round. You were working with other people and you could have conversations, jokes and whatever. And this was very pleasant. But now unfortunately that's a thing of the past.

Then when you'd done this and the hay was actually dry, they used to have a big thing called a sweep, which was like a horizontal comb consisting of long wooden teeth, about ten, twelve foot long, with spikes on. And this would be driven on the ground, on the front of a tractor, to push the hay up to where the rick was being built. And this was built by putting the hay into an elevator which took it up, deposited it, and then my job – it was always the boy's job – when this stuff comes off the elevator, is to stand and pass it to the man that's building the rick. This is quite a skilled job. And you get covered in all the dust and bits that come off the hay, but it was not that unbearable. Again, very sociable, because there was quite a few of you working at that point. And as the Irish say the crack is good when those sort of things are happening. And they bring down tea or cider halfway through the afternoon, and it's pleasant. I did enjoy my time working for Mr Doggrel.

All mod cons But the funny thing was about the landlady. She had this beautiful bathroom suite in this old farmhouse, which she showed me. She said if I wanted a bath, to give her a couple of hours notice. I couldn't understand why, but then again I didn't think about it. Anyway on the Friday I asked if I could have a bath. She said, Yes, you'll have to give me an hour or so. And apparently she needed the notice because although she'd got this immaculate bathroom suite, I think it was salmon-pink, there was no plumbed water, she had to boil it all up in buckets and lug it up the stairs to the bloody bath.

But nevertheless, she made me very comfortable. She was very chatty, there was no sort of problem me being fifteen and her being I suppose in her late seventies. I think the fact that I wasn't a boozer – couldn't afford to be a boozer, apart from my age – made me acceptable, because I think previous lodgers had been drunkards or something like that. But I liked that woman. Of course she's gone now and a few years ago we drove past there and I found they'd actually demolished her old farmhouse, but I'm not surprised, it was very old. And thatch is very nice on postcards, but thatch to live in is very noisy, the amount of things that live in that thatch and run around at night, and every night, is incredible.

She had just cold water and one tap. She had electric, because she was very proud of her radio, an old wooden cabinet radio. There wasn't a plumbed-in toilet. It was a bit embarrassing, because she gave me directions where the toilet was, it was an outside loo down the garden, but it took me three days to find it, I found it easier to go up into the woods to perform my bodily functions. I did find the toilet eventually, and it was just a bucket-and-chuck-it type job. Well she obviously had a cesspit.

Goodbye to Doggrel's   But I enjoyed working for that man. I think I must have been there about three months at the most. It ended because Mr Doggrel – he'd told me from day one – was moving to another farm, but unfortunately there would be a period when he was without a farm altogether. He was going to rent a house or something, with his family, so obviously there would be no place for me. So when the time came for him, just before he was shutting down the farm, I went back to London.

I was still under the YMCA contract, yes. I think they were a bit miffed because I didn't write and ask them for another placing. But I'd got a bit cheesed off with the YMCA by this time. Although Mr Doggrel was all right I didn't know what they were going to put me into next.

Van boy   So I went home off my own bat. That was the first time. I got a job as a van boy for a while, with the Advanced Laundry from Wealdstone, near South Harrow. In those days lorry drivers had mates and van drivers had van boys, usually fifteen-year-olds that would do a lot of the leg-work. This was during the time of the London smog, when there were real pea-soupers. I remember on some occasions having to walk with one hand on the wing of the van, and then feel my way along the kerb so I could shout at the driver, tell him when he was getting too near the kerb. I mean it's hard to imagine being able to do that these days, with the amount of cars parked, but at that time it was possible. It was incredible.

Great Hampden   Then I got notification from the YMCA that they'd heard about me moving from Doggrel and found me another place, with a Mr Buckingham in Buckinghamshire. Yes. He was a tenant farmer in a village called Great Hampden, near Great Missenden, on the Earl of Buckingham's estate.

The farm was only about a hundred acres and I think he had eight cows and a few bullocks. There was myself, the old man who I'm sure must have been in his late seventies, he was very old, and a woman called Miss Jackson who was a left-over from the wartime Women's Land Army days. She was housekeeper-cum-farmworker. And her and I did not get on.

The old man was very bad in his legs anyway. On one occasion we were cutting thistles round the field. I was driving the tractor, he was sitting on the back of this old-fashioned mowing-machine operating the blade and he fell backwards off the machine and hurt his back. Which meant he was laid up, I think, for eight months. And I had to milk the cows then. And I didn't miss one milking for a year. That meant twice a day for a whole year.

Milking   Now this was handmilking. I wasn't really shown how to do it, but the first day I was told to sit under a cow, and just get hold of her teats and milk, squeeze. Eventually I did learn the proper technique whereby you don't actually squeeze, you play, a bit like a flute, going with your index finger, then the next one down, so it's like a rippling motion. That's how you do it with the cows that have reasonably sized teats, but if you've got a heifer, she has very small teats and then you squeeze it. And heifers are usually real bitches, because they're not used to milking, and they kick and play up. You get the situation sometimes whereby you might have half a bucket of milk, and she's lifted her leg, tried to kick you, but put it back inside the bucket. So you've got to retract the leg from the bucket without losing all the milk.

But handmilking is quite a nice job in the winter inasmuch as you've got up what seems to be halfway through the night and it's cold and it's dark, and you snuggle up against the cow and you soon get used to the smell, it's not too bad a job. Summer-time's not so good because they're swishing their tails to keep the flies off and a slash from a cow's tail, invariably covered in cow-crap, can be quite an unpleasant experience.

Prickly idyll   Mr Buckingham also grew corn, because I remem-ber harvest-time. When I look at these picture postcards or paint-ings of the harvest and it all looks romantic, with all the stooks, the stacks of wheatsheafs lined up, it looks romantic, a bit, what's the word, idyllic. But the reality is that when you actually have to handle these things, you pick up a sheaf under each arm and stick them together so they stand upright. But, this is in the days before everything was sprayed with God knows what, there was obviously lots of thistles and all sorts of nasties, so your forearms, if you had your sleeves rolled up – and don't forget this is August time, you'd be hot – your arms would be full of thistles from these idyllic-looking sheaves of corn.

Huntin', shootin' & beatin'   My first meeting with the hunt was in the village, and there was all this lot of horses and people and God knows what. And I was wandering round looking at them, thought, Yeah, I've seen it all before on Christmas cards.

Then I was confronted with two young madams, who I don't think were much older than me, and one of them said in a very toffee-nosed voice – and it's quite easy to look toffee-nosed when you're up on top of a horse looking down on someone – Hold my horse my good man. Literally in those words.

With a Roedean accent. I couldn't believe it. I looked up, I said, Do what? And she said, Hold my horse my good man. I said, Stuff ..., I didn't say Stuff you, because that wasn't fashionable, I didn't use an obscenity, but something that she had not encoun-tered before, because I think she almost whinnied like a bloody horse. That was my first confrontation with the hunt.

Another thing that used to happen there was that on Saturdays in the shooting season the Earl of Buckingham would have a pheas-ant shoot, and various farmers were asked to release their boys on Saturday to go as beaters on these shoots. And whilst it wasn't compulsory, it was expedient for a tenant farmer to release his boy for Saturday, so I duly went and joined this group of villagers for this beating, this shoot.

Again it was quite interesting. There were an awful lot of nobs there but for all the price of the guns a lot of them couldn't shoot. I've seen pheasants almost fly down the barrels of these guns and they've still missed the bloody things.

And the object was that you walk in a line, and the game-keepers, they're like regimental sergeant-majors, they keep the line straight. It's important that you keep the line, and you move when he says, Move, and you stop when he says, Stop. And the older village hands knew exactly what was what and where we were going, and they used to make sure they were in the right position, whereas the inexperienced lads would find themselves going through blackthorn and blackberry bushes. But you had to go through everything, without any hesitation, and do exactly what you were told, so we used to get torn to pieces.

Another strange phenomenon was that often, if you were in thick cover, birds wouldn't be found. But that night, if you went in those woods, you'd bump into all sorts of villagers that were there collecting these birds that couldn't be found, sly devils. I suppose that was one of the perks.

But it was quite interesting, it was a day out, it was mixing with other people, and you got ten bob and a glass of beer and a sand-wich at lunchtime, and the Earl himself, in all fairness, was very pleasant. I don't know what the expression 'No side' means ex-actly, but he didn't seem to speak any differently to us than he did to these friends on the shoot. Which was OK.

Chasing girls   The farm was near the village of Great Hampden, so at this time I did have a bit more of a social life. I chummed up with a couple of village boys there and we used to roam round the countryside chasing girls and one thing and another.

There was a girls' boarding school at Great Hampden, I don't remember the name. I think it was situated in what used to be Hampden House, which was a very old place, I suppose a manor. Obviously they were well out of reach, but they did employ maids there, I think Irish and some foreign. And we used to go and hang around their accommodation in summers, in the dark evenings, but we never got anywhere of course.

I also joined the Young Farmers' Club at Great Missenden at that time, but again it was a bit of a one-sided affair in fact be-cause all the others were farmers' sons or daughters or pretty well-placed people, I mean quite well off, and I didn't exactly sort of fit in there, and the fact that I'm a Londoner, and made no apologies for that fact.

But I desperately wanted a girlfriend. Hence the lonely hours listening to Jo Stafford on the American Forces Network. I don't think I ever actually cried at that time but I know that I was very lonely, very lonely. And it would have been puppy love.

Puppy love Did I have crushes on girls when I was adolescent? Oh God, yes, yes I did, oh dear, yes.

When I was working with Mr Buckingham I had a girlfriend that I'd met in London. She was a very intelligent girl, I think she was going to a girls' grammar school at the time. Quite tall, quite attractive, still at sixth form and judging from where they lived, and the house and the father, I'm sure they would have been middle-class. And I was a farmworker, so whether I was the equivalent of a bit of rough, I don't know. I didn't make rustic grunts or have straw hanging out of my mouth and cowshit on my shoes all the time.

It was talk mostly, and go to the cinema, discuss books, discuss politics, an awful lot of talk, more talk than snogging. Talking about politics I suppose, a lot of the time. Our reactions to what was going on. And moaning about our parents, I mean most teenagers spend an awful lot of time getting uptight about the restrictions put on them by their parents and how embarrassing or stupid or domineering they are.

I was madly in love with her and I missed her terribly and I couldn't think of any way of getting home. I wasn't owed any time off or anything, and they depended on me for the milking. So I thought well if I broke my arm, then I'd have to go, that's it. I was looking for a blighty wound. And the way I tried this, it was so stupid – we had massive barn doors there, double doors, and I'd noticed that if you opened them and there was a wind blowing they would come with one hell of a crash. So I opened this door, ran back in, put my arm in the part where the door would close onto, and the wind brought it down and it came down with a hell of a bang. I tried it twice, but all I got was a bloody awful bruise. It didn't break. I was that desperate to get home and see this girl. It was so stupid. But it wasn't my right arm, I'm not that silly.

Romance   It was consummated, I remember, up against the bloody garage door. It was funny because when I got home that night my stepfather said, Have you been drinking? And I hadn't been drinking but I was obviously looking quite knocked out, one way or the other. Because of this, for want of a better word, knee-trembler against the garage. That was I suppose my first really proper physical experience.

Yes, that was good. But the romance didn't last very long. These things don't. Absence didn't make her heart grow fonder, in fact it just went the other way, so that fizzled out. But at the time it was the grand passion. Incredible.

I tended very much to fall romantically in love with whoever I was infatuated with at the time, I mean passionately. Whether it was because I hadn't felt there was any love in my own childhood, I don't know.

Old Tom   We also had an old horse on the farm and I loved that horse, the only animal, I suppose, that I ever got badly upset over. This old horse, his name was Tom, and the reason the old man had him was an arrangement with the local knackerman, that if a horse came in to be knackered, and was not totally knackered, to coin a phrase, the old man could have him for light work, like pulling a cart and things like that, with the understanding that when he'd finished with the horse it would go back to that knackerman.

So we had old Tom and I soon learned to harness him and work with him. It only involved usually light harrow work or just pulling a small cart with stuff on the back. And on Sundays I used to ride this horse bareback, with just a bridle made out of baling string, round the farm to check the fences for the old man. And somehow or other, I think because I used to give him a few lumps of sugar or something, that horse would always be available and easy to catch on a Sunday and in fact sometimes would come to the gate. But other days I'd go up to catch him for work, and he would play hell. One of his tricks, he would get up behind a group of heifers in a field and they would disperse, and then he would come at me at full gallop, and believe you me a bloody cart-horse weighing the best part of half a ton, coming at you at the gallop ... I never called his bluff. I don't think he would have gone over me but I always jumped out the way. And it was this sort of ritual every blooming morning that he had to go to work, catching him. And once he was caught he was OK, he wouldn't play up at all. As I say I really did like that horse.

I had worked with a horse before, with Mr Doggrel, I'd done hayraking. But that was a very fit, strong white horse – or grey, as they're called.

Anyway, I remember in the spring being sent up this field to check the horse, and Tom was laying down. Well, there's a problem with old horses, sometimes in the spring they lay down and they can't get up. If they get up they're OK. So I went back down the farm and I said to the old man that Tom's laying down in the field and he can't get up. So he said, We'll have to try and get him up. So myself, the old man and the housekeeper-cum-farmworker went up to the field. I got a bridle on the horse, so the old man had that to hang on to, the woman, Miss Jackson, got hold of his head and I got hold of the rump end. He knew what we were trying to do and was struggling to get up, but every time he struggled he moved his head – any horse that gets up, whether it's a racehorse, a donkey or whatever, always moves its head to give it the lift to get on its feet. But every time he did this the woman panicked and let the head go, flop back down again. And in the end she just convinced the old man that it was futile, we couldn't get him up, it would be kinder to have him put down.

So they sent me back down to the farm. They'd rang up the knackerman, and I heard the gun. They shot him. And he was pretty old anyway, but that's not the point, I would rather not have been there, or part and parcel of the failure to get him onto his feet. Because I think if there'd been another man there, or someone that wasn't scared, we'd have got him up. And I did cry over that.

Bolshie   I think Miss Jackson regarded me as bolshie, because when seeing in the papers industrial disputes or one thing or another, I'd expressed some sympathy when I thought it was justified. The other thing which was quite funny, I used to have the *Reveille* delivered then, and it would invariably have a scantily-dressed pin-up on the front. It would be very tame stuff now, I don't think there was any topless in the *Reveille*. But this woman would really take me to task over this. I think she regarded it as an obscene publication.

I remember one occasion when the vet was there, he was in the kitchen washing his hands, and I'd come in from milking, was having my breakfast, and they were talking about the latest strike, I can't remember who it was, what it was over, and they were discussing this with great indignation. And she actually made a statement, Oh I think these union people should be shot. That was her actual words.

After I'd fallen out with her over Tom, I just couldn't even be civil to her at all. I didn't like the woman anyway. And in the end the old man said, Well there's one or the other of you's got to go, Peter, and you can't cook. That would be only a month or so after Tom was put down. So again I got the chop.

Woolies   I came home again, and had to get a job straight away, virtually, because my parents wouldn't let me leach off them. I got a job as trainee stock manager at Woolworth's in South Harrow. I lasted there a couple of months, and then I got another letter from the YMCA to go to another farm.

Abingdon   This one was in Abingdon, Berkshire, right beside the River Thames, in fact some of the land actually bordered on the Thames. It was a weird arrangement. Barton Court, which used to be a sort of small manor house I would imagine, was a nursing home where people of modest means placed relatives that had become a nuisance, or embarrassing – dotty Aunty So-and-So or incontinent Uncle Whatever. It was that sort of place.

And there was one other boy, a London guy, Tony from Brixton, that was working there when I arrived. He'd been through the YMCA training scheme, but not in Somerset. He'd gone to the one at East Grinstead which was run on different lines, more like agricultural college lines, where they actually had days of not working, but days of lectures and things. Tony became my mate.

We actually lived in the attic of this nursing home, and were kept separate from the patients. There was one other person that worked a bit on the farm, this slightly retarded old guy, but he couldn't be relied on to do much. He was quite sad. He was affable enough and we used to bung him the occasional fag. He would stick it in his mouth, and he wouldn't take it out till it was finished, and it would just stay there and burn, I don't think he even inhaled it, but he liked it.

The other person on the farm was the manager, a man I think in his thirties, who I am convinced to this day was mad. He tried to run the farm on fairly modern lines, namely we had a tractor, with hydraulics, and quite a bit of machinery. I was taken on there principally because by this time I was over sixteen so I had a provisional driving licence and could drive the tractor on the road, whereas my mate Tony, who did the milking, was fifteen and he couldn't drive a tractor on the road.

Skiffle   We were ten, fifteen minutes from the actual town of Abingdon, which was a town I liked very much. It was a market town, and quite interesting, there's lots of old buildings. And there was a bridge over the river and walks though the meadows, which was where everybody promenaded on a Sunday, where you used to go and look at the girls and the girls eyed the boys, and that sort of thing, which was quite nice. And this is an era, I can remember quite distinctly, when skiffle started. It would be mid-fifties. And we used to get a skiffle group, with a tea-chest bass, in the local café or coffee bar we used to go to. Which was quite good.

I didn't like this particular farm manager very much, in fact I got quite abusive with him when he tried to fiddle me over a dinghy Tony and I wanted to buy to take out on the river. And then he found an excuse for sacking me, a couple of weeks later. Something was unsuitable, insubordinate, whatever, and that was it, I got the chop.

Sausage factory   So then I went home again, and this time home I worked in a sausage factory which was situated in the industrial estate in Wembley, close to Wembley Stadium.

My job was to take any imperfections out of the fat, and any bits of skin that the machine hadn't taken off, because it was a perfectly flat machine. And I used to have to remove things like cysts, and on some occasions there were bullets in these pigs. Now I couldn't understand what bullets were doing there. I've since been told that the MOD has used pigs for testing various types of live ammunition. No one obviously will admit to that, but I think that's where these pigs may have come from.

I stuck this part of the factory I suppose for a month, and then I was promoted to the assembly line, which involved chopping up veal, putting it through this massive mincer, and various other things and weighing them in their component parts. It was part of the section which made sausages for tins of pork and beans, which is why I never eat them. There were quite a few Poles working in the factory, and also quite a lot of Irish guys. This was my first contact with Irishmen and I somehow struck up an affinity with them straight away. I liked them, I liked the carefree attitude, and if something was wrong, they wouldn't just tolerate it, whinge about it, they'd either jack or have a row with the foreman, tell him exactly what they thought or whatever. I quite liked this forthrightness of them.

Bully   Also it was the first contact I had with someone that was overtly gay. I remember an incident, one particular guy at this factory was a real bully, he used to rag this young guy – I think he was about seventeen or eighteen – about being gay. This young gay guy had got quite a nice racing bike, and we were coming away from the factory one night, past the ornamental ponds there used to be on Olympic Way I think it was called, or is called, on the way down to the Stadium. We used to walk up that way to the tube station. And this bully got hold of this gay guy's bike and threw it in this pond. And one of the Irish guys come up behind him and shoved him in after it, and wouldn't let the bully out of the pond until he'd groped about and found the bike. And that put the end to that bit of bullying. Again the Irish shot up in my estimation. I know it's ridiculous to base a liking on one person, but that just seemed to me typical of the guys there, which was quite nice.

What's in a sausage?   The other thing I remember, from my first few days there, which was very disconcerting, was having to run the gauntlet of about seventy or eighty women in this section of the factory, and of course when you're young and callow like I was, there were sort of remarks that these women would make, and what with that and the job they were doing, which was filling up these sausage-skins, with the sausage-meat coming out of the machine, which was very phallic, I used to get very embarrassed.

And the sort of stuff which went into these sausages was incredible. I remember one Friday when I think it was about a pound or so of apples went into one, I'd got this pack of green veal and questioned the quality of this veal to the foreman, and he said, Ah, bung it in. And someone else's identity bracelet fell in the machine, and a bit of my thumb that I'd chopped off inadvertently. And this was all in one batch of sausages on a Friday afternoon.

Again, the smell of the place was awful, and the fact that it was inside. And I was really surprised by the standard of hygiene, or lack of it. I saw a Health Inspector come in there once, and he didn't come anywhere near my section. From what I can remember he went straight upstairs to the offices, went to the boardroom, and then came out about two hours later and went out to his car. So that was my only experience of a Health Inspector in that bloody factory.

I didn't particularly like the job but I earned reasonable money, I suppose, more than I'd earned on the farm actually, but I just didn't like working inside. I suppose I was earning about six, seven quid a week then. And on the farm I'd be lucky to be earning four, or three.

And it meant commuting to Wembley from where I lived, from where my parents lived, in Rayners Lane, South Harrow, on the tube train. Quite a few youngsters working at the factory used to get the same train, and one particular guy thought it very funny one day to have a bag of pigs' eyes and throw the pigs' eyes around the inside of this very crowded tube train. Which didn't go down too well with the commuters and the secretaries, etcetera.

Intensive farming Then I got a letter from the Abingdon farm manager, asking me to come back. They were going to give me another chance, and all this business. When I got back – because I wanted to go, I liked the town and got on very well with Tony – it turns out that Tony had said that he would pack the job in and go if I wasn't taken back on. And they relied heavily on him, I mean for a fifteen-year-old boy to be virtually totally responsible for milking twenty-five cows and looking after them – well he was getting a few bob over the top but not much, he wasn't paid a man's wage – he was a very valuable asset, which is why they begrudgingly took me back. And then a couple of weeks later they took on another two boys, so there's four boys on this farm now, all under seventeen.

And everything went along fairly smoothly for a bit until he started this wild idea of getting more milk per acre from the meadows. And this was the plan, that he would graze this field, beside the river, with an electric fence, moving the electric fence up a few yards every day, so the cows had to eat what they were given, instead of wandering and picking up bits like cows do. Cows are very wasteful eaters when they're just grazing an open field. Then two of us had to spread nitrochalk, which is a fertilizer that makes grass grow artificially quickly, on the grazing that was behind the electric fence.

Now in those days no one mentioned anything about pollution and nitrochalk going in the watertable or in the river, but obviously it did. And he would have known that. Also he bought these whacking great irrigation guns, the sort of thing you see on market gardens and fields in Lincolnshire. They go round and round, spray water and irrigate a large area. These were going twenty-four hours a day. They were fed by a pump that was pumping water straight out of the Thames.

He then got the four of us together and said, Right, now you know we're doing this irrigation thing, I want two of you to move those guns during the night – he called the irrigators guns – so two of you will be on nightwork. So then I piped up, How much extra are you paying for nightwork? So he said, I'm not paying anything extra for nightwork, your hours start from Monday morning, seven-thirty, till twelve o'clock Saturday. It's a forty-seven hour week, I dictate what hours you work in that time, so. And I said, No way. I'm not going to do it. So then the others who were present, who I think would have backed off if he'd taken them individually, but he hadn't been crafty enough to do that, they couldn't very well say anything else but, No they wouldn't do it. So the idea was scotched. Plus the fact that he had to shut the whole thing down anyway because the Thames Water Conservancy didn't like it.

An agitator & a communist So at the end of that week I was sacked, and he wrote a note to my parents that I was sacked because I was an agitator and a communist. Those were his actual words. He didn't tell me that, that's what he wrote to my parents. He told me that as I was being uncooperative, they couldn't use me and this time I had to go whether Tony went or not. I wasn't given anything in writing, no. He was a nasty piece of work.

SUSSEX BY THE SEA

Bright new world   So that's when I moved south. I'd been given a week's notice from the Abingdon farm, which they had to give, so I wrote to Brian, a pal of mine who had moved from South Harrow, just round the corner from where my parents lived, down to Hove in Sussex. This would be summer 1956, when I was rising eighteen.

I think his father was some sort of a builder, a bit of an entrepreneur, to put it politely. He'd been arrested for being involved in an armed robbery. He didn't take part himself but I think one of the people asked him to look after some stuff, whether it was the actual cash or not I don't know. Anyway he'd got put away for a year, and Brian and his mum had moved down to Hove. I wrote and said, Could they put me up for a while till I got sorted out down there, as I was going to be out of a job at the end of the week? I got a letter straight back saying, Yeah, yeah, come on down.

Which I did. I told the farmer I was going and he assumed I was going home, because I'd been home before. I was laying like a false trail, I didn't want anybody to know where I was.

So then I rolled up in Sussex. Caught the train down to Hove, fine Saturday, typical Sussex day, really nice, very bright. Walked with two bloody great suitcases from Hove Station to Portland Road which was quite a walk. And found my mate's place in Portland Road, his mum had a greengrocer's and they lived above the shop. At the time – it was one of the few jobs he did have – he was a projectionist at the Embassy Cinema along Western Road, it's inland from that art deco block of flats, Embassy Court. You come straight up there from the sea-front.

And anyway I sort of kicked my heels in Brighton that first night, waiting for him to finish work at ten-thirty, eleven o'clock, and then we just started going round the various coffee bars, which were numerous at that time, it was wonderful. And I fell in love with Brighton straightaway, I thought this was an absolutely super place. We didn't get home till about three that morning, because there were places open, and lots of people about, which

I'd never experienced anywhere before. I mean, I liked Abingdon, but there was not any night life after the pubs shut. Or the Saturday night dance which ended at twelve o'clock, which was a bit like a village hop. But in Brighton and Hove there were lots of places open and all sorts of interesting-looking characters.

I just thought I'd reached the epitome of sophistication, decadence. It wasn't quite Berlin 1930s but it was my equivalent. Especially when I saw a guy came in – and this must have been before the homosexual Bill – actually quite openly carrying a handbag and being as camp as you like, you know, this was a knockout. Brighton has always been a place for gay guys anyway and I was impressed that the town itself seemed so tolerant and I think that was a very very important thing to me.

Brighton boats   Why I fell in love with Brighton was partly because I'd never spent much time by the sea at all and I thought it was fantastic, all the paraphernalia and the amount of fishing boats that were actively working full-time off Brighton beach, and the fish market which was still down on the beach itself, which was fascinating.

I also used to walk along the sea-front to Shoreham, usually a couple of times a week, and in Shoreham itself there used to be a very old boatyard, I think it was called Suter's Yard. That was downstream from the Norfolk Bridge, behind the small parade of shops which is there now, next to the Bridge Hotel. And it was full of really old boats. I can just remember the kind of black and dark-timbered vessels, and remains of vessels. Unfortunately there was a fire some years later that rubbed the whole lot of that out and it was developed, which is now I think where the present Labour Exchange stands. That was really a step into the past, I was fascinated by that.

I never thought at the time that I would have any sort of boat myself. I didn't think it was within my range, I wasn't earning a lot of money, I didn't know anybody with boats anywhere, it was just like a daydream. I used to fantasise sometimes, but I just didn't imagine how wonderful it would be to go on one of those boats or go fishing.

Fruit & veg market   One of the contacts from my friend's mother's shop got me a job on the Brighton veg market in Circus

Street, as a porter. I think I started, not on the Monday, but a week later. This was quite heavy work, but well within my capabilities. It was heavy because I was spending half the night out in Brighton and then getting up at five to go to work at half-past five in the morning at the market. I was picked up in a van by someone coming through. I worked down there for a few months.

What you do, you're actually loading up the various green-grocers' vans or lorries when they pick up produce from the stand where you are. The market is divided up into various owners and my employer's name was Mr Stoner. Anyway after that initial rush is on you get various other jobs, and one job that I had to do was to take sacks of prime cabbages from this flat-bed Lincolnshire lorry, and empty the sacks, one by one, into the Council tipper-lorry to take away rubbish, and this was going straight up to the tip apparently, because the prices were not good enough. To maintain the prices to the greengrocers this stuff was thrown away. Nothing wrong with it at all. Nothing wrong. I remember that quite clearly.

I used to get the *Fishing News*, the commercial fisherman's newspaper at one time, and now and again you'd get an article in there about lorry-loads of prime codling which would go for fish-meal because the prices weren't good. I mean, that is a crime. I thought, why not offer these prime cabbages to some old people, give it to a hospital or children's home. But no, no, up to the tip.

There was a driver who'd been ill, I don't know what was wrong with him but he was not too strong, and occasionally I had to go out on the lorry with him and help deliver stuff to the various greengrocers' shops out in the sticks, out in the rural areas. It was quite nice, I got to see a bit of Sussex, and again it was more riding than lifting, which I quite liked.

Downs bungalow Then my mate's father was due to be released in a month or so, and I think his mother then decided, or it was part of the plan, to sell the shop, and move. So the shop in Port-land Road was duly sold and we moved – myself, my mate and his mother – to a bungalow in Mill Hill Drive on the outskirts of Shoreham.

As I've said, I'd been to Shoreham before because sometimes, during the evening when my mate was working as a projectionist, I walked along the front all the way through to Shoreham and the harbour, and I found the harbour fascinating. I'd not had anything to do with the sea but for some strange reason I'd always had this interest in boats, ever since my little yacht with the yellow plastic sail.

The bungalow was part of the development that was creeping up to the Downs, very slowly. It was a complete contrast to the flat over the shop in Portland Road. It was a cul-de-sac and at that time the back garden just backed onto fields and a really good panoramic view of the Downs. It was really quite nice. If you looked due south you could see the soapworks chimney in Shoreham, and the old power-station, which had just been completed, and the sea of course. So you had quite a view. Very pleasant, very quiet. If you came out of Mill Hill Drive, left took you back down to Shoreham and right took you actually up onto the Downs, where there was nothing except fields and gorse, and onto Mill Hill itself. And when you went up to the north, you got to a point there where you could look back right across the Adur, Shoreham Airport, the sea, and that vast valley. That was before the Shoreham flyover, so there was no big road scar, just lanes leading north to Steyning and Beeding and places.

And the A27 going over the old wooden toll bridge, which was in full use. They had two guys there that collected sixpence a go. I used to go over there on my motorbike and flash back behind them, because I think they were making quite enough money. I heard the rumour that they'd made enough each to buy a house. I don't know if that's true, it would have taken an awful lot of sixpences. But it seems incredible now to think that that bridge took lots and lots of heavy traffic.

And the railway line went through there, along by the river, all the way to Horsham, quite a modest old steam train. That's now become a cycle track, which is a good use for it anyway, but that's quite pleasant. The line was maintained up until ten, fifteen years ago just to serve the cement works. They used to take big trucks in there with the material for the cement, and take cement out. But it ceased as a line right through to Horsham many many years ago, it must have gone with the Beeching cuts, yes.

Brian's dad We'd been there a month or so and Brian's father was released and came to live at the bungalow.

He was very much a go-ahead sort of chap, he couldn't be kept down. And very soon he talked himself into this job as a manager of an engineering works, when I know for a fact he didn't have any formal engineering training or qualifications at all. In fact I seem to remember I had to write out his references. Anyway he got a job in Horsham.

Nye's Farm   When we moved to Shoreham I obviously didn't want to have to get to Brighton Market at that unearthly hour in the morning from even further away, it was bad enough from Portland Road. So I went to the Shoreham Labour Exchange to see what they'd got, and they sent me up to a Mr Nye whose farm fields were immediately at the back of the bungalow. The actual farmhouse was just off the Old Shoreham Road. It was called Nye's Farm then, but the old name is Little Buckingham Farm. That's all gone now and the valley is absolutely filled with a Wimpey housing estate.

He took me on as a casual harvest worker, and my particular job was to ride on top of the combine, and as the corn came out

5. Nye's Farm (Little Buckingham Farm), Shoreham, looking west along The Avenue, photographed in the late 1950s not long after Peter worked there, and shortly before demolition of the buildings.

of the chute, I had to bag it up, big sacks weighing two hundredweight, two hundredweight and a half. And these were then slid onto like a ramp which was part of the combine. And when there was four or five sacks there they would be put onto a trailer. But you'll understand, this is when this thing's going along up on these hills, and you're quite high up off the ground, and it was quite a job to maintain your balance and handle these bloody heavy sacks. They were heavy, my God. And you couldn't stop, I mean stuff was coming all the time, so you had to keep up, you know, you were geared to the speed of the machine as it were. Which happens in a lot of situations.

The days were very long when the weather was good, obviously you'd got to keep going. I used to sometimes come home half-past nine, ten o'clock at night. You didn't get paid an overtime rate because you were casual. And if it was wet, then he wouldn't need you for the day, so you wouldn't get paid. Luckily that summer the weather wasn't too bad and I didn't lose too many days.

As far as my lodging was concerned, I think the amount of money I was giving Brian's mum for my keep just about covered the food. They weren't making anything out of me, which was a blessing. They were very kind people. I mean whatever other people may think of his criminal activities or whatever, they were kind to me, so I've got nothing but praise and gratitude for them.

When the harvest finished Nye decided that as I was fairly useful he would take me on full-time as permanent staff, which meant that, although my money wasn't good, I had a regular wage coming in, I wasn't losing time. And if I did work overtime then I would be paid for it. But I did rather resent the fact that all those hours and everything I'd worked as casual, he could have been taking me on permanent then. But he didn't, obviously. Typical farmer.

I was doing general farmwork. I'd collect the eggs and help with the milking if one of the cowmen was off. One of my jobs was to feed the turkeys. He kept quite a few turkeys, and they were kept in this dovecote. Now when one normally thinks of a dovecote, it's this short thing on top of a pole. But this dovecote was a building, I think it was flint-faced, or flint-built, and was quite large. Thirty, forty, fifty feet across maybe. And is still there to this day, just off the Old Shoreham Road, where Nye's Farm used to be. I'm pretty sure there's a preservation order on it. And it was massive. I don't know when it was built but it was obviously quite old.

Bagging a brace of chickens   And after a month or so I was going to visit my mate Tony in London, the guy that I'd worked with on the farm in Abingdon, who was back home in Brixton living with his mother. And they were pretty badly off so I thought, I can't go up there without taking something. I hadn't got any savings, I'd got my fare just about and that was it, so I thought, I can't go empty-handed, what I'll do, I'll pinch a couple of nice chickens. And on the way back to the bungalow one lunchtime, I was going up this field, because the chickens were roaming about all over the place, they were free-range, literally. I grabbed two hens, wrung their necks quickly, and I was in such a panic I pulled one of the heads right off.

Put them in the sack and ran up the field, thinking I'd got away with it. And the sack was jumping around like a live thing. Anyway I thought, Well that's good. I took them into the bungalow, plucked them and did all the things, Brian's dad helped me, he hadn't started work by this time.

Anyway a couple of days later I was working away up in one of the other fields and the shepherd, Gordon, came up, he said, There's two of your mates from London down to see you, they're waiting in the barn down below. So I thought, Oh that's funny, I wonder what's up then. So I went down to the barn and walked in, and directly I walked in I knew they were no mates of mine, they was these two very obvious coppers in plain clothes. And I'll swear one of them had navy blue trousers on and big boots on, big feet, I mean you know, the absolutely stereotypical sixties-type plain clothes copper.

Then followed the usual – though not usual to me – rigmarole, We would like you to come down to the station to answer a few questions, you know what this is about, etcetera. Although the journey to Shoreham nick was a short one it gave me just enough time to figure how I would handle this turn of events. And first of all I thought of denying everything. I thought, No one's seen me, I haven't told anybody, other than Brian's family, and I knew they wouldn't say anything. Then I thought, No, because if I do that, they're going to start snooping round. And what I was really scared of was that Brian's dad might have been on parole, and I did know enough about parole to realise that anything at all could send someone back inside, and I thought, Well I don't want that. I wasn't frightened of him, but it was just that it would be an awfully silly thing to do on my part.

They started asking me questions and I admitted I did steal two chickens. And they said, OK we've got that, now what about the eggs and the cabbages. I said, Eggs? And the copper says, Yes, so many gross of eggs, or whatever? I said, I haven't had any eggs, how the bloody hell could I steal eggs, I haven't even got a bike. And obviously someone had been having stuff away wholesale, and they wanted me to admit to everything: you've admitted to the chickens, why not admit to the eggs and the cabbages or anything else that's gone? Make life easier for you, get it off your chest, etcetera. And I was adamant, I said, No, I would admit to and take the punishment for anything I've done, but you're not going to lumber me with all that, no, no way. And they kept on for about a couple of hours, this is in Shoreham police station. And then they gave up and thought I was being stubborn or whatever. But they fingerprinted me and let me out on police bail. I wasn't a sort of arch-criminal, I wasn't a threat to society or anything.

I think they did know I hadn't taken the other stuff, but they wanted to make it all very tidy. So obviously I told Brian's family what had happened, and that I'd admitted it and everything else, and his dad said, Thanks very much, that's all right, there's no reason for them to come here. I'd got the chickens and taken them back.

Mugshot   I was due to appear at Steyning Magistrate's Court on the Monday. And I went to Steyning, and when I got there the police said, Right you've got to come with us for a minute. I thought, Oh what's this? There's a pub immediately on the left as you come into Steyning village, the White Hart or the White Horse, it's still there to this day. The car park fronts, but it's elevated, right on the High Street of Steyning. The police had got a white board set up there, and I had to sit in front of this and have my photograph taken, face on and side view, with a number in front. Which I thought was awful. There's no way today people would tolerate that. And this was for their criminal records. Right in public view, right on the street. But again, you know, who could I appeal to who would say anything?

So then I went to court and played the most contrite act I've ever performed, said it was just the spur of the moment, explained why I wanted them, and I was given a bit of a lecture by the magistrate and given a conditional discharge and fined eight pound and that was it. And was lucky to get out.

I didn't want to involve Brian's family at all and I was a bit scared when I went in the court, because I thought, I'm living in digs, I don't have any family, no one's sort of come and spoken up for me, saying that I lived a sort of reasonable life and it was steady and I was with responsible people – which I was, in a way. I thought they might give me some sort of stupid custodial thing to put me on the straight and narrow as it were.

So I came back from the court, and Brian's dad said, Well I don't think Mr Nye's going to take you back, he probably doesn't believe in criminal rehabilitation. And in fact after I'd been arrested I didn't see Nye again. He sent my money up in a brown envelope, I didn't actually ever speak to the man again.

I can't feel too bad about it, but if I'd been in his shoes I probably would have confronted the person that had stolen from me, not just handed it straight over to the police like that. And he must have sussed out, I would have thought, that I couldn't have been the person stealing his eggs and cabbages wholesale, it was someone with a car, and I think I was one of the only people that didn't have a car, for God's sake.

Machine operator   So Brian's dad, who was by this time manager of the works in Horsham, said, You can come and work at my place. That was in the winter. So I started work and Brian was working there as well. When we'd moved from Portland Road he'd given up his job at the Embassy Cinema and I don't remember him getting another job at all, until this one in Horsham. My mate Brian was not very good at getting a job or wanting to go to work.

I was working a capstan, which was just quite a mundane sort of job. The machine was set, in other words it was repetition, making up components for bits of aircraft engines. It's not even down to your own judgement, you can only wind the thing in so far, then it stops. The cutting tool will not go in any further. The man that sets this machine up is the really skilled man, a bit like a computer programmer is today. So it didn't need an awful lot of skill, or concentration for that matter. Initially I found it quite interesting because it was something I hadn't done before, and the money was a lot better than I was earning on a farm. And the other guys, and there was a few women in the factory, were pleasant and friendly enough. But I only stuck it a couple of months. I wanted to be outdoors again.

Mostly hoeing   So I got a job with a Mr Clow, a market gardener, who had fields in I think Small Dole, but most of his work, where I worked, was in a field behind Southlands Hospital. That same ground now is a Council housing estate.

The work there was pretty boring. It was mostly hoeing. He also employed quite a lot of women there. And they were good fun, they were cheerful, I mean even with back-breaking work, they used to manage to chatter and laugh, and even sing some of the time. And I did have admiration, because most of them had families and husbands and houses to keep as well and the work was quite hard. It was boring, but they used to just get on with it and didn't seem to take any notice of how boring it was. I've seen woman doing that sort of work before, in factories and stuff, they could cope with it much better than I could, or men can.

I noticed one or two practices there which would be frowned on very much today, like for instance, we used to throw ordinary washing soda, spread it along the lines of carrots. I don't think it made the taste better, I think it was another way of forcing them. I stayed there a few months. And he noticed that I didn't like hoeing, because I remember him coming up once and saying, Oh hoeing isn't your forte, thinking I wouldn't know what forte meant, and I said, Well no it isn't, because I find it bloody boring to be quite honest, I said, but that's it, it's a job.

A little eccentric   Then I heard that a farm in the area, now this is coming up into midsummer 1957, would take on boys for the harvest and pay them a good rate, overtime as well as a wage, and didn't lay them off, and that they were earning really good money, as far as farmwork was concerned. And this was just three or four miles from where I was living. I decided to go up and see this man one evening to see if I could get a job there. So I walked to this two-thousand-acre farm one evening and met this Mr Freely. We had a chat and he said I could start work in a week's time which would give me time to give Mr Clow my notice. Of course Mr Clow asked me why I was going. When I told him I could earn more money he didn't believe me and seemed to resent my going.

Mr Freely was a little eccentric. I discovered later that one of his little quirks was that he would pee anywhere, against your leg if you didn't watch him. He wasn't a yokel-type farmer, he wasn't a straw-chewer, but then on the other hand he wasn't a gentleman either. He was odd, very odd.

Corndryer   My job was to work in the corndryer, situated in the big barn. What used to happen, he had a combine that used to cut the corn, not the type I'd worked on at Nye's, and the cut corn was stored in the combine until it was full, and he used to buy these ex-Council dust-cart lorries, not the modern ones where it's all hydraulic at the back, these were the old-fashioned ones where they used to slide the sides up and tip the stuff in off their shoulders. He would bring these alongside the combine and they would empty the combines into these, and these were driven by fourteen-, fifteen-year-old boys. You can imagine it, I mean kids being allowed to drive things like that. And then they were driven up to the barn, as fast as these things would go, I think he tried to govern them, I don't know how successful he was, but I know there was a lot of wrecks and crunches.

And they would tip this corn into the pit, where I was working, and then this was taken up with a series of elevators into the actual corndryer, a big container which hot air was blown through. The hot air was supplied by a coke-fired furnace, and the heat was blown through with fans.

After some time in the dryer the corn, which was was mainly barley, went through a series of drums which separated out the chaff. Then it would come down through a series of chutes in various sacks, the good stuff and the rubbish in separate sacks. And we had to take it off of these chutes, weigh the sacks accurately on scales and then wheel them and stack them. We also had to keep the furnace stoked and take regular moisture tests. On top of this the machinery, which was mostly second-hand, kept breaking down, and the corn kept coming relentlessly.

There was two of us working in there. And the sacks were weighed off at two and a quarter hundredweight, again very heavy, very heavy to handle. All right when you were on the ground, wheeling them with sack-wheels. But we had to stack them, two of us, and even two of you lifting those, they're very awkward. And when the lorry came in we had to carry them, on our backs, and stick them on the lorry, that was damn heavy, that was damn heavy, that was two and a quarter hundredweight.

One of Mr Freely's endearing habits was to pee on the coke that we used to stoke the furnace with. Now coke fumes were bad, but coke fumes combined with hot urine, it was almost unbearable. I really did remonstrate strongly with him over that, I didn't like that, I thought that was ridiculous. I said, Is it absolutely essential that you pee on the coke when you come over to the barn? I think those were the words I used.

Bang!   The nice thing about working up there, there was a lot of boys, I think maybe six or seven at the time. And of course we were up to any sort of nonsense that was going on. We had to do moisture tests on the corn, we used to take a sample of dried corn every so often, put it in this pressure container, and put a measured amount of carbide in. Well carbide reacts to moisture, and that would give the percentage of moisture, acceptable or unacceptable, in the sample that we were testing. But we also found out that if you put a little bit of carbide and a droplet of water in a Tate and Lyle's treacle tin, and hammered the lid on, it would go off with one hell of a bang. And we'd done this one day, with this tin, and the old man, Freely, rolled up, and we thought, Oh Christ. And we'd put a very minute drop of water in so it would take a long time to go. And he's lecturing us about something or other, standing with his back to this thing, and it went off with an almighty bang and he nearly leaped out of his suit. And the most amusing thing about it, he said, WHAT THE HELL WAS THAT? And all of us, to a man, said, What? As if nothing had happened. And none of us flinched or jumped.

Time and motion   Another thing with him, some misguided fool bought him a stop-watch for his birthday. And he was timing everything. I used to roll my own cigarettes at the time, because I couldn't afford tailor-mades, and he stood there one day timing me, and he said, How many cigarettes do you smoke a day? And I can't remember what it was, twenty or thirty or whatever. He said, Do you realise how much time a year you spend rolling your cigarettes, how much time you're costing me? He said, Couldn't you buy tailor-mades, or roll them up at night before you come to work? I said, No, I can't, I said, I'll buy tailor-mades if you'll give me the equivalent rise. Anyway I did hear later on, though no one would admit to it, that somebody stamped on that bloody stop-watch and we didn't see any more of it.

It was very hard work in that corndryer. It was running day and night six days a week, seven days some weeks. A couple of times I actually worked right round the clock. By God, was I tired! But I did earn good money.

We hated handling barley. When it's ripe and the dust is flying about there are minute barbs and when you sweat they get into the pores of your skin and drive you mad with itching and the more you sweat the more you itch. It drives you absolutely mad. And even after a couple of baths, you can still feel this stuff, apart from getting in your sinuses and everything. I can remember actually rubbing my back up and down a brick wall because it was driving me so mad, this irritation.

Mix-up It was mostly barley we were drying, because Freely's fields would not grow good quality corn. With barley there's different grades. For brewing barley it's got to be top-notch, or seed-barley even better. And the same with wheat, if it's going to be used for bread, it's got to be top-notch, or it's just used for animal feed if it's second-rate. And none of his stuff was good enough quality. But he used to do contract drying for other people. Other farmers would send lorry-loads of stuff up and we'd dry it. On one occasion another farmer had sent his corn which was superior to that of Mr Freely, but Mr Freely sent it to the merchant's as his own. Well, anyone can make a mistake. And when Freely's dried corn was sent in under the farmer's name, it was inferior quality. But the other farmer didn't go for it at all, he knew damn well that his stuff was grade one. There was quite a row and I don't think we dried that farmer's corn ever again.

County crawler Finally the harvest was finished and Mr Freely asked us to cut our hours to the minimum. I was eighteen at this

6. Peter in his twenties.

time and on a man's wage, seven pounds a week, which didn't leave much after I'd paid my digs and HP on the bike I'd bought, besides which I was now courting seriously.

Now I'd finished operating the corndryer I became a tractor driver. And I was driving what they call a County Crawler, which was a big, powerful tractor on tracks, like a tank, ideal for working on the steep sides of the downs. Because wheeled tractors roll over, in fact I think today that's still the thing that causes most fatal accidents on farms. The big drawback for me was that it had no cab and believe me, when the wind was coming from the north-east it was bloody cold. To this day it makes me shiver to even think about it. But what I used to do, if I was doing something that was not precise – now ploughing is precise, you can't muck about with that, you've got to keep your eye on what you're doing all the time – if we were rolling, or harrowing, I used to put the tractor in gear, get off and run beside it to keep warm. Most of his fields were pretty big and then I'd jump on again before the end, turn the thing round, face it up the other way, and then get off and run beside it again. Just to keep warm. It was dangerous because if you didn't get it right you were under the roller or the harrow and that could have been really iffy.

If you're sitting stationary and you've got the wind, I don't think you can have enough clothes. If it rained, you had a sack and you poked the corner in and wore it like a monk's cowl. I didn't seem to think it was such a hardship at the time but looking back and making comparisons with how things are now, I suppose it was. But I being young and silly, or macho, it didn't strike me as being particularly hard or tough.

Bachelor pads   Then Brian's parents sold the bungalow at Mill Hill and moved to Horsham, to be nearer the factory that he was now managing, another factory. But I had nothing to do with that, so I suppose my life sort of shuts down as far as that family are concerned, at that time.

I initially moved into a really seedy place, a one-room so-called flat in Clyde Road, Brighton, near Preston Circus. The house reeked of stale gin. I think that was the landlord and landlady's tipple, it was awful.

I was commuting to work on this mobilette moped which belonged to the farm, part of a sort of pool of transport he had, bikes and things. And this bloody thing used to conk out, I used to pedal it more than use the motor. And I got really fed up with that, and of course the rent was a big lump out of my seven quid a week farmer's money. Plus the fact that it was an awful long way to go to work.

So I stuck it out for a few weeks in that flat and then told Freely I was cheesed off with travelling. He said, Well I've got a house in Gardener Street, Fishersgate and you can rent it for a pound a week. So I gave my notice in to the landlady at Clyde Road in Brighton and took over this house. It wasn't a tenancy, he was just going to stop me a quid a week out of my wages. It was a very small terraced house, it's still there to this day.

Radar towers   When the winter ploughing was done, Mr Freely had got another bright idea. He'd bought four radar towers. They were built just before the war, and they were at Hindhead, which is on the Devil's Punchbowl, near Haslemere. And he'd bought them because they were made of timber, which he was going to sell. I heard he'd paid eighty quid each for them. I'm pretty sure they were two hundred and twenty foot high. Well, there was an awful lot of timber in a two hundred and twenty foot timber tower, an awful lot of timber. But he had to dismantle them. Or we had to dismantle them. And I was sent up there in a lorry with another guy, to start this dismantling business. And I must admit it was scary, two hundred and twenty foot is pretty high. I had no training whatever in this sort of job.

The only occasion when I wasn't nervous was climbing the tower to replace the red aircraft warning light. I'd had a motor-bike accident in which my glasses were broken, it was a misty day and when I'd climbed a fair way up I couldn't see the ground. It was a combination of mist and myopia.

The way we did it, we put a massive steel hawser from the back of the lorry over the top of the tower, and down the other side, onto the tractor winch, which I was driving.

We walked out on the beams, no harness, undid the pre-war nuts and bolts and fixed a section to the steel hawser. Then bring the lorry back, wind the tractor winch in and lower it down. And it was pretty scary, especially as this was winter, and that gets bloody cold up there. Often the beams were white with frost.

They were nine-by-fours, on edge, with blocks in between, so you didn't have a very wide thing to walk on. You had one foot on one four-inch bit, the other foot on the other four-inch bit, and you waddled across like a duck to get to the legs of the tower where you were undoing these things.

Then the other guy got married, and said he wouldn't go up any more as now he was a married man he'd got responsibilities. I think he lost his bottle, quite honestly, but then again I didn't blame him for that, because the way we were doing this job was dangerous to the point of lunacy.

So then Freely took on another guy, a local man, and I'm sure he wasn't doing it for the seven pound a week that I was getting as a farmworker. Anyway he carried on working with me dismantling this thing. But then Freely came to the conclusion that the way we were doing it was taking too long, so he then came up with the bright idea of taking the towers down in thirty-foot sections. Which involved putting the hawser on top of the thirty-foot section, cutting through three of the legs with a chainsaw, or undoing the fishplates of three of the legs, and then pulling this section with the tractor winch, as well as doing the other business.

And on one occasion, we'd got it all winched up, and I'd started to wind in, but something happened, I don't know if the wind blew or what, and the section went back the other way and lifted the whole lot – me, the tractor, the lot – off the ground. That was an instant laxative, it really was.

On another occasion, we'd started to pull another thirty-foot section, and the hawser parted up near the top where it was connected. So muggins had to climb up ninety foot, up this bit where we'd sawn the legs through and started to pull it, and re-fix the hawser. And again I was very shaky, doing that. I got away with it, we pulled it down.

A bit on the side We dismantled all four. And we did a bit of flogging of timber on the side if we knew the old man wasn't there, and a bit of hardcore. There were two of these towers at one end and then another two about two hundred yards apart. And there were the buildings that went with it, where they had all the instruments and electrical stuff, and I was rooting around in one of these old buildings once and I found this cable sticking up, massive electricity cable, and I think there were six of them altogether and I thought, I wonder where that's from. And I discovered that it ran

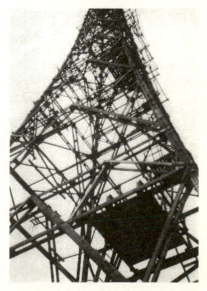

7. *One of the timber radar towers at Haslemere, dismantled by Peter working with one other man, probably in the winter of 1957-8.*

the two hundred yards up to the other radar towers. So in other words there was maybe twelve hundred yards of this really heavy duty cable. They were lead-wrapped, with big copper cores, that's good scrap money. So I said to the guy that drove the lorry, Look, we've been flogging this that and the other just to make a bit on the side, there's this cable, why don't we have this, the old man doesn't know anything about it? It was in ducts and you could have pulled out whatever length you wanted at a time. But the lorry driver was too scared, it was just too much money, he wouldn't do it. So that's still there to this day.

I was very aware of how much I wasn't getting paid for doing this job, even though I pointed out to Freely how dangerous it was, and it wasn't sort of part of a farmworker's remit to work as a steeplejack. I heard later that a firm of steeplejacks wouldn't tackle the job, they wouldn't have anything to do with it. So, I'd no conscience.

But we didn't have the cable and that little episode came to an end. That lasted quite a few months. Without mishap.

Exploitation   But to counteract being scared, there's this macho thing, that, well, I can do it. Plus the fact that you get it from other people, and usually from employers, Well, can't you do it then, are you scared? And you do it, in spite of common sense and logic, you go and do something which is dangerous and which does scare you and which really you shouldn't do. But nevertheless you do it, especially when you are eighteen.

Which is why I resent the fact that they're cutting eighteen to twenty-one year olds out of the minimum wage. Now this is an age where employers really exploit people, because they know that these kids – and you are a kid at eighteen, I don't care what anybody else says, even though you're regarded as a man – will do almost anything. And I know that at this age I was most exploited. Are they exploiting the young man's need to prove himself whilst paying him lower wages? Yes, that's exactly what they're doing. Why do they recruit guys in the army at eighteen, or younger, that's all part of it. Looking back on what I did on those radar towers I realise that if it wasn't for this machismo thing that young men go through half the wars in history would not have been fought.

'Sacked' by Freely So Freely got all his timber out, and there was a lot of timber. Then it was coming up to harvest time again and he said, I want you to operate the dryer for me again this year, Peter. You did it last year and you did it well, you stuck it. He promised a good bonus if there were no breakdowns. What a joke! The machinery was the same as the year before. I knew I wouldn't have much of a choice, but I really didn't want to do it, because I'd been outside all the winter, it'd been very cold a lot of the time, working in really bad conditions, yet when the good weather came I was going to be stuck inside the poxy dryer. But I thought, Oh well, it's a job.

The first load of corn that was coming in was from another farm. And he said, There's a lorry coming in this afternoon. I said, Well, I've arranged to meet my fiancée in Brighton at a specific time, and I want to knock off at five-thirty, my proper time. So I'm warning you now, if that lorry's not here, I'm not going to wait for it, or whatever, it's got to be here. He said, Oh no, no problem, it'll be there.

So I waited. Four o'clock came. No lorry. Half-past four, five o'clock. I rang him up, because there was a phone connecting the barn to the farmhouse, and I said, The lorry's not here yet. He said, No, it will be there, don't worry, it'll be there. Anyway five-thirty came, no lorry. I rang up and said, There's no lorry Mr Freely, I'm going now, I did warn you. He said, No, you've got to stay there, you've got to be there to see that lorry in, to unload and everything. So I said, No, I've told you. If you go, he said, you're sacked. I said, Well that's as maybe, but I've told you. But anyway I've waited till quarter to six, the lorry didn't come, so I flew home, didn't have any dinner or anything, got changed and went into Brighton to meet Wendy. That was on a Thursday.

So I took the next day off and went and got myself a job on a building site in Fishersgate, Rice & Sons. Anyway I went back up the farm Saturday, because we worked Saturday morning anyway, and I said, I want my cards please. He said, What for? I said, Well you sacked me. He said, No I didn't, that was a misunderstanding. I said, It wasn't a misunderstanding on my part, you told me that if I went – and I went after my official knocking-off time by the way – you'd sack me. I said, That's it, I'm sacked. He said, No, no, no, no. He said, It's just the heat of the moment Peter, don't, you're not sacked. So I said, Well, I am sacked. I said,

I want my money and my cards. So he gave me my money, which was in the form of a cheque. And he wouldn't give me my cards. He said, No, you think about it over the weekend, you'll feel different on Monday. I said, I can assure you I won't. But he was adamant, he wouldn't give me my cards.

So I finished with Freely on the Thursday and started with Rice's on the Monday.

Farewell to the farm This ended my career in agriculture. I was still only twenty. I don't regret the time I spent working on the land. I worked with some very fine men who even in this day and age deserve a much better deal than they are getting. As for some of the people that employ them, I have more respect for their animals.

BUILDING HOUSES, ROARING ABOUT & STARTING A FAMILY

Hod-carrying   When I started at Rice's it would be the end of the fifties. The job was knocking down two streets of houses in Fishersgate, very small houses, before they were going to build some houses and flats, which is what's there now.

After I'd been working with Rice's a month or two, a chap I'd met a couple of times, called Dan Horgan, came round to the Fishersgate site and said, How about coming and working with me, more money and we'll have the crack. I then went hod-carrying with him for a firm called Boyd & Cozens. Dan had to show me over the weekend how to load a hod up with bricks, I was that green. Normally if you're hod-carrying you start off on the ground. But we were what you call three lifts, three or four lifts up, in other words we were up to the second storey of this block outside Burgess Hill Station, shops and maisonettes. So on the Monday, we went up in the back of a lorry to this site.

The work involved filling the hod up with twelve bricks and then going up the ladder. It was terribly difficult. You've got to find your balance, and hold this bloody thing, and all the rest of it, and be able to step off the ladder without losing the hod, or losing it over backwards. Which I managed. The only thing is, my shoulder was so sore, it really was sore, because as you take it off it catches your shoulder, until you get the knack of half throwing it off. No pad, Oh God no, that would have been frowned upon, I mean you just wouldn't do it. Too macho. I survived and my shoulder eventually got hardened. But it did bleed, and it was hard going. Always the same shoulder, I always carry on the left, even though I'm right-handed.

And what particularly annoyed me was that there were three or four other hodcarriers, working round the other side of the building, but they were loading up wheelbarrows, pushing them onto a platform hoist, and there was another guy on the top taking the barrowload of pug or bricks off the hoist. They were paid as hodcarriers as well, but paid more than us two, although they never put anything on their shoulders. They were blokes in their thirties and forties. That did annoy me. They were getting paid more but not carrying, they weren't beasts of burden like us.

Brickies   In my day, it was usually a ratio of two brickies to one hodcarrier, but sometimes we were looking after more than that, three or four. We were running all the time, and I mean literally running. My mate Dan was very powerful. He could pick a hod

8. *The brickcleaners, April 1961: Dan on the left, Peter in the middle, Brian O'Connor on the right.*

full of bricks up with one hand and put it on his shoulder. Now that's heavy, I could never do that. But I got reasonably profi-cient, and it didn't take me too long before I could actually let go of the hod. Because when you go up a ladder you don't actually hold the hod handle, you have to balance it. But it took me a little while to find out, if I went opposite leg to opposite hand up the ladder, then you remain in reasonable equilibrium, you didn't sway about, whereas before, when I was trying to go up holding the hod as well, I used to sway all over the place.

Some brickies are shouting for bricks all the time, you get some right awkward so-and-sos. When the bricklayers start working on internal walls, you'd have them all over the place and you might forget some of them. We had one really awkward Yorkshire bloke and he was working inside this maisonette. What he would do, he would go all day if necessary, and if no one came near him he wouldn't shout for any bricks or pug, but if the general foreman or the brickie foreman came, he'd start hollering. So we thought, Right you so-and-so, we'll fix you. So what we did one day, Dan and I, we loaded up his scaffold with so many bricks and so much pug he couldn't even get off the thing until he'd worked his way through it. And there's him, with ten minutes to knocking-off time, trying to get rid of all these bricks and this pug. He left us alone after that.

We used to go to work in the back of a lorry, and that was bloody cold. It had a canvas top, but nothing at the back, and it was steel-floored and your feet used to get frozen. We didn't treat the work like it was hard. It was hard, but we used to laugh and muck about, and there were another couple of youngsters working there.

Working for Evershed   After working for Boyd & Cozens for a couple of years I got a job with another builder who was part of quite a well-known Sussex family over at Peacehaven, called Evershed. He persuaded me to go self-employed and he paid me more than I was getting on Boyd & Cozens. He would come in sometimes – his actual trade was a chippie – but most of the time he was sort of somewhere else.

He was OK, Ron Evershed, nice guy. He'd have manic fits and scream and shout. One of his favourite sayings was, If we're going to have a fuck-up, let's have a royal fuck-up. He was not your conventional builder at all, he was an ex-Navy man and his sole claim to fame as a matelot was that he'd served on the most heavily bombed destroyer in the British Navy to survive. We'd get yarning lunchtime, because I found out it was a good way of getting a long lunch-break, get Ron yarning about his Navy days.

Hussein   And I was working with a coffee bar friend of mine, Hussein Cotwal, an African Indian, who was the bricklayer, and we were working out at Littleworth, which is a hamlet adjacent to Partridge Green. Just the two of us, building and knocking down houses for this builder, Evershed.

A nice thing happened there. We used to walk to the station at Partridge Green, this Asian guy and I, to get the train back to Brighton. And this was still the same steam train that ran from Shoreham to Horsham. And we were walking up this lane one day, it was quite a walk to the station, and this woman was coming down, she'd got a nipper in a pushchair, a toddler. And he was looking at Hussein, the kid had obviously never seen anybody dark before, and he's pointing, and the woman was getting dead embarrassed, and she said, Oh I'm very very sorry. Hussein said, No, he said, it's all right, he's never seen a black man before. And he was really cool, he said, Come on, touch my face, look, and let the kid touch, which I thought was really wonderful.

Hussein's dead now, he died a few years back. His widow Cynthia lives up the road, and his daughter comes to our house quite a lot. I've got great time for them. I like Afro-Caribbean people, the ones that I've met. I've known Cynthia for forty years, she comes from Guyana. And he was OK. He'd had a bit of racism of course, I don't know any of them that haven't, quite frankly. I know that her sister, that used to live I think it was at Moulsecoomb, had to park her car about a mile or two away from her house because it was constantly vandalised by people, and racist slogans all over the bloody thing.

One-man demolition   Then Hussein went back to Africa and I was virtually working on my own. What Evershed was doing was knocking down a cottage and putting up two, or a bungalow. I virtually demolished one place entirely on my own.

And what I also did was clean the bricks. Which was another laborious, very boring job, but it saved him a lot of money, because it was cheaper than him buying bricks and he could put up what was there before. He used those bricks as face bricks, so that would be approved by the planning people. And I could clean maybe two thousand, three thousand bricks a week, which was a hell of a lot.

Switch the dem thing orf!   One Saturday, I'd worked the morning at this hamlet near Partridge Green, and was on my way home.

At that time I had a motorbike, I think it was called a DKW or a DMW – it wasn't a BMW, definitely not – it was only about a one-fifty, but it was such a pathetic, weak bike, and it was a two-stroke. Now two-strokes are notorious, they'll start perfectly OK from cold but if you've been running them for a while and they stall, they can be a pig to start. This one was a particular pig, once it got hot. I'd left the job, and about a hundred yards down a lane, the hunt was coming down and it was a lot of horses, dogs, and people.

Anyway I didn't want to stop the bike but at the same time I didn't want to cause any problems with the hunt. So what I do, I throttle it round down to almost stalling speed, and then walk the bike through the hunt, until confronted by this red-faced pig, who shouted at the top of his raucous voice, SWITCH THE DEM THING ORF! That's exactly what he said. So I thought, Well you ..., anybody can see I'm doing my best to cut the noise to the minimum. So I just opened the throttle, jumped on it, slung it into gear and roared through. And there was bloody dogs and horses flying everywhere. I've no regrets because anybody could see I'd done my best to try and avoid startling the horses. But he still wasn't satisfied with that, but it just was the arrogant Switch the dem thing orf, that I just took exception to. And that was my last dealings with any hunt.

Progress Then, when Evershed had completed the work at Littleworth, he got other building work in Heen Road, Worthing. He bought I think three houses, and part of a terrace, and our job was to knock these places down and he was going to put up a restaurant or a supermarket or something. By this time Hussein was back from Africa, and it was him, Dan, myself and another guy, who were working for Ron.

I worked for Evershed a year or two, then I was with various other firms. Altogether I must have worked about five years in the building trade, as a hodcarrier and labourer, from about twenty to twenty-five.

Motorbikes Ever since I'd left home I'd wanted a motorbike, because the places I was living and working in were very isolated for the most part.

When I moved to Abingdon, I'd kept contact with some of the

guys at home and one of my mates had a Velocette, a very old bike with girder forks, and I think I bought it off him for a fiver. It was quite an old wreck, but it went, and it gave me more mobility. I don't think I *went* very far on the thing, but it was nice being able to roar about on a motorbike, as much as you could roar about on an old thing like that.

I then sold that and bought a beezer, a BSA two-fifty, which was a much more modern bike and it had telescopic front forks I remember. I got that on HP and I was well pleased with it. I actually rode to London a couple of times, as well as driving round Oxfordshire, and at one point actually rode past the house where my mother and stepfather lived, as an act of defiance as much as anything.

When I moved to Shoreham I had quite a few different motorbikes. One I think was a Norton, with a hand gear change converted to a foot change, which was a real pig of a thing. I could only get first and third gear, which was absolutely bloody useless. In fact I got so frustrated with this thing that I threw it in a ditch on the way to the farm I was working at and left it there. That was the end of that one.

Then there was the best bike I had, a 500cc BSA Star Twin, quite a powerful bike at the time. I was working all the overtime hours God sent on that farm, on the corndryer, that's how I managed to raise the deposit. It doesn't compare with nowadays bikes but then it did seem very powerful. And I really loved that machine, even though it did try and kill me twice.

I never wore a crash helmet and I very seldom wore gloves. They weren't compulsory then. I should have done but I was so stretched financially I just couldn't go to luxuries. I had a sort of a PVC jacket, which would absorb a lot of the superficial grazing if you come off and skid along the ground, and jeans tucked into wellingtons. On mornings when it was very wet and I had to ride to work, I'd get there and empty half a pint of water out of each wellington. I used to have wet feet all bloody day. I wouldn't put up with it now, but I just didn't use to think anything of it.

Spring fever   I did have one girlfriend on the back of that, Gloria. I had a brief thing with her. But when I was engaged to Wendy, I got rid of the bike, someone else took it over. That was the last of my decent motorbikes.

When I was working for Ron Evershed I got that DMW, the one I was riding when I had the confrontation with the hunt. Then there was a Royal Enfield, I think that was a three-fifty. But they were just a means of getting over to the job, because the train was expensive and not very good.

But for years afterwards, every spring, I used to get the urge to have a motorbike again. Even now I think I look a bit enviously at people with bikes. It's the freedom. Total freedom. And being independent of anything or anybody. I think that's the thing about a motorbike. I've never had a car. I don't believe you can get that same feeling with a car. You can literally just get on it and go, theoretically where you like. You can stop where you like, it's easy to park. And of course there's the image, the sort of biker image, to a degree, although I never really came into that category, I mean I never had a leather jacket or any of that nonsense. But there is an element of that. It's more macho on a motorbike than sitting in a Ford Prefect. Definitely.

As for speed, whichever bike you've got, if it's a fair-size bike, you've got to do the ton at some point, which I did. I think I did it on the A23 somewhere, which was the A23 then and not the M23. It's hard to imagine and I can't remember which particular bit I did it on, because it's all changed so much, but I definitely did a hundred miles an hour at one point. I had to do it at least once. You have to.

One occasion which was quite funny, I was coming along the sea-front from Shoreham to Brighton, and I flashed past one of the roads leading onto the sea-front, it might have been First Avenue, or Grand Avenue, one of those, and just too late I noticed the Old Bill were sitting there in a patrol car. I thought, Oh Christ. And I saw them pull out and the blue light go on, but luckily there was quite a bit of traffic. I then got in front of a stream of quite close traffic, bumper to bumper virtually, tucked myself on the inside and the Old Bill went flying past at about eighty mile an hour and I got away with it. But I watched my speed after that, because I just couldn't afford the tickets.

A little bit crazy   Wendy never rode on the back of any of my motorbikes. She didn't object, and she quite liked being on the back of motorbikes, she'd been on the back of bikes before. But I knew that I was a little bit crazy, a little bit reckless, and I really didn't want to have an accident with her on the back, or kill her or whatever. Like a lot of guys of my age, I used to be pretty mad, quite fast, and I'd overtake in dangerous positions.

Wendy It was in 1958, when I was still living at Mill Hill and working for Freely, that I'd met Wendy. I tended to be hanging around at the Espresso Lounge in North Street and that was where we met.

The impression I got, which was part of the attraction, was that she put on a sort of Nothing-shocks-me face, an attitude of I've-seen-it-all-before. I didn't know then that this is partly to cover her shyness. She wasn't sort of outgoing or bubbling over like some of her contemporaries, in fact she didn't fit in any category. There was something enigmatic about her, I felt there's more to her than meets the eye. I found her very attractive. Still do.

Probably the initial attraction for her was rumours that I was not too civilised, to put it mildly, and I'd just come out of prison. It was the dangerous thing and that often works with women when they are young and impressionable. I think they soon grow out of that. And I didn't belong to any particular group that she would have been familiar with.

9. *Wendy, Newhaven Harbour, 1960s.*

We got engaged after a week.

Wendy was living at home with her father and younger sister. Her dad was working nights, so I used to stay the night at their house off Lewes Road, go off in the morning before he came home from work at seven o'clock and walk back to Mill Hill. That would be about five miles. Sometimes I would be on the settee, making out I'd missed the one-eight train back to Shoreham and he would give me a lift up the station.

Espresso fight The Espresso Lounge was above a couple of shops, a very popular rendezvous at the time. One Saturday night, a couple of weeks before I moved to Fishersgate, we had met in the coffee bar and were going on somewhere else. As we were leaving, there were two blokes standing outside the doors on the upper landing. Wendy knew them. They said something and sniggered. I turned back and asked them what was so funny. One of them said I had better shut up or he would close my other eye. I started to see red (with the eye that wasn't closed) but Wendy pulled me away and asked me to ignore the fool.

I brooded on this and didn't get a proper night's sleep for a fortnight. Wendy remembers that I was unbearable. I was determined to settle it one way or the other.

A fortnight after the first incident we went to the Espresso again and this guy was there. I went up to him and said, Right, you, outside. His answer was that he was not going outside and that as he was doing his National Service he was sick of being pushed around. He then made a dash for the stairs. I rushed after him and jumped over the bannister from the top landing to the ground floor while he ran down the two flights. Why I didn't break a leg I'll never know, it was real Errol Flynn stuff. I got to the doors leading out to the alley and bolted them before he got to the bottom stair. I then grabbed him by the lapels of his jacket and rammed him up against the wall, then hammered at his face with my head. He tried to avoid punishment by tilting his head back as far as possible but it didn't do him much good, it just meant his teeth took a severe battering. So did my forehead. I then threw him against the other wall and proceeded to punish him with my fists. I felt his whole body crumple and knew it was all over for him.

By this time a crowd of people had come down the stairs from the coffee bar to break it up. Wendy had kept them at bay until I had finished him. I stood back from the guy and said, OK, I've finished. The other people picked him up, unbolted the doors and hustled him out. As he was going through the doors I jumped forward and punched him behind the ear which sent him spinning up the alley.

I have no regrets about hitting this individual. He made the opening play and the very silly mistake of underestimating someone. In hindsight I'm pleased that at the time I didn't have a weapon. I am sure I would have used it.

I've been involved in a few memorable scraps, before and since. And some others, but they didn't amount to much. I don't think there is anything particularly clever about fighting but I do know there are a lot of people and situations where reasoned argument just doesn't apply. I also know how very badly I've felt on the very few occasions when I have backed off from a confrontation.

Wendy and I went to the cinema after the fight, but the blood kept dripping out of my head which I'd really opened up on this guy's teeth. After we'd come out of the cinema, because it wouldn't stop bleeding, we went up to the Sussex County and I had my head stitched up. And then I thought I'd better go home.

Cockroaches   That was the night I moved into Freely's house in Fishersgate. I'd never been there but I'd got the key to this place. I walked, it's about five miles I suppose. I'd got rid of the bike by then. I'd got a sleeping bag and a few belongings in a rucksack, found the house, had to find the number on the door with a match. This is about one in the morning.

And went in. And it was funny because there was nothing in the place. The electric had been switched off, when the house had been unoccupied. Just, it was all echoey and bare floorboards, and smelled musty. So I put the sleeping bag on the floor, got undressed, God knows why, took everything off except my underpants, went to sleep. And when I woke in the morning I felt absolutely dreadful, my head was absolutely pounding, it was a real bad headache. After you've been in a fight all the pain from the muscles you've used comes through the next day. And then when I took in my surroundings, there was this dingy bloody empty cottage, or house. And I sort of looked around and then my eyes gradually came down and I looked on the floor, and where I'd been walking in the night, I'd squashed all these bloody cockroaches with my bare feet! And that was one of the low points in my life I think, that was bloody awful.

But anyway I moved into this house, and one consolation was, there was a bit of coke left in a bunker outside and I could have hot water and I used to have a bath. I gradually moved some old junk furniture in, and Wendy used to come over with food, sort of semi-prepared because she knew I wouldn't bother to cook anything even if I did have facilities. I stayed there a few months, while I was still working for Freely. The cockroaches seemed to disappear, or I didn't see them, or I didn't want to see them.

Landlady When Freely sacked me obviously I had to leave his house in Gardener Street and I then moved into digs off Middle Road in Shoreham.

There were quite a few lodgers for the size of the house and the room I was in was shared by two others. We were so cramped that we had no wardrobe in which to hang our clothes, these had to be hung on the picture rail or kept in our suitcases under our beds. When I first moved in I was working on demolition which is a very dirty job but the landlady only allowed us one bath a week, so on some evenings I used to go and wash on Kingston Beach at Shoreham Harbour.

After a time Dan left home and moved in to share my room. One day we came back to the digs very early due to bad weather. We got home about eleven o'clock, we got washed and changed and we were going to go into Brighton. I asked the landlady what was the earliest we could have dinner, as normally we had it at seven in the evening. She said, You can have it now if you like. This was about 11.15 am. I then realised why the meals were so awful. They were cooked early in the day and then left to congeal till the evening.

Things came to a head when she took a white sweater (without asking me) and shoved it in the wash. It came back like a skin-tight vest. When I confronted her with it she said it had a fault and that I should take it back to Marks and Spencer and exchange it. This sweater was bought as present from Wendy, my fiancée. I duly took the sweater back to Marks and saw the manager who was very apologetic but said he could not change it as it was patently obvious it had been washed at a very high temperature. I told the landlady what he had said and that I thought she should replace the sweater. This she refused to do so I told her that one way or the other she would pay for it.

The following evening when she was at bingo Dan and I put our belongings in a big tin trunk and lowered it out of the bedroom window so none of the other lodgers saw us, and took it into the new digs we had got. We returned for that night, Friday, and went to work as usual the next morning. We normally paid our digs money after work on Saturday. Of course we never went back.

She knew which site we were working on and informed the police that we had bumped her for the rent. When I was questioned about this I said we had paid a week in advance and as she kept no rent book she had no case, plus the fact that if she made too much noise the Inland Revenue might start asking awkward questions. I'd warned her she would pay for the sweater!

Lucky strike The new digs I struck lucky. This was with Jean and Jack Bartlett in the Upper Lewes Road. They were a really nice couple and I was happy with them. Best digs I ever had. Ironic that I only found them a few months before getting married. I realised that living as a lodger with a nice married couple was quite a good solution for a young single guy.

Wedding I had my twenty-first birthday when I was working for Boyd & Cozens, then Wendy and I got married. I asked for a week off, I said I was going to have a week off for our honeymoon. We got married on the thirteenth of February, 1960. Good thing it wasn't a Friday.

The wedding was at Brighton Registry Office, in Prince's Street. The guy that I'd like to have been best man, Dan, couldn't and wouldn't do it because he was afraid of the paperwork, because he's dyslexic. So a mate of mine, Peter Maywell, came down from London. But Dan organised, got people into taxis, not that there were many of us. It was a bitingly cold, sleety day, and we went back to Wendy's father's house, and there was only half a dozen people there.

We'd moved in to a basement flat in Clifton Terrace, owned by people that Wendy had worked for. Very nice couple. One reason I never went back to farming was that as a married man I feared the insecurity of living in a tied cottage. Not that we got a lot of security, as it turned out.

For our honeymoon we went to the pictures, and the highlight was going up to London Zoo. Then I got a message from Cozens that if I didn't go to work the next day, I wouldn't have a job. That was it, had to go back to work. So it was a three-day honeymoon. But I worked for Ted Cozens for I think another year after that.

España In 1962 we were still living in Clifton Terrace and my friend Brian said, Do you fancy going to Australia? I've got this car, a big Mercedes, quite an old one, and we've got the caravan. I'm getting married, we can go if you share the expenses. By this time Wendy and I had got our son, Mark, who wasn't much more than eighteen months old. I talked it over with Wendy and we thought, Well, we're not achieving much here, we're living in a flat, well that was fair enough but it wasn't very special. We fancied the idea, and said, Yeah, why not. My mother and other people said it was a terribly irresponsible thing to do when you've got a child. But I knew that people had been round the world in yachts with very small children, so we'd give it a go. I'd never been anywhere abroad at all.

So I asked my mother if she'd lend me – not give but lend – thirty pound. She said no, she wouldn't. Wendy – this is the bit I really feel bad about – sold some jewellery she'd had from her mother, who had died just before we met, to raise x amount of pounds to pay for our share of the food and whatever. So I jacked in my job, it was with Darkie Warren, a subcontractor for Braybon's. We gave up the flat, and drove down to Dover in the car and the caravan, with my mate, to go right through France. The idea was that we'd go to Spain first of all, because he'd been to Spain and liked it, and then see how it went from there. Round the Med and down to Africa, eventually. Then, once we got to the Horn of Africa, we'd obviously have to ditch the car and the caravan, and see how it went. I would, or we would, work any opportunity anywhere, doing anything we could. This was supposed to be the first step towards emigrating to Australia.

Innocents abroad   We actually crossed the Pyrenees from Biarritz, the widest bloody part you could imagine, and the worst possible route as far as mountains were concerned. I remember sitting in the car, and it was dark, and literally craning my neck right round and looking up and thinking, Christ, there's another road up there. And it was a hairpin bend. I'm sure if we'd have done it by daylight we wouldn't have attempted it, the roads were so steep.

Anyway we crossed the worst of the mountains by night, went through a place called Logroño and then the car packed up. It just wouldn't go. We managed to get the caravan off the road, and this was just miles from anywhere, in the foothills of the Pyrenees. So, what are we going to do? We've got no Spanish, we didn't know anybody or anything. Talk about innocents abroad. It was a Sunday, so we knew there was nothing going to be got sorted out anywhere, and we all stayed there that day. But on the Monday Brian managed to hitchhike a lift with his wife, into the town, to try and arrange a breakdown truck, mechanic, whatever.

The breakdown truck took the car back into Logroño, about as big as Horsham. They took the car into the garage and then, rather than leave us out in the middle of nowhere, they said that all the time they were working on the car the caravan can be parked on the garage forecourt. And we were in the town I suppose a week because they had to send to Germany for a spare part, the differential had gone.

So there we were on the forecourt and we used to go shopping down the town to the supermarket. There was no beach or anything, but every day was an adventure, you were walking round, seeing. We were stared at, I don't think there'd been any tourists there.

Village hospitality   So they fixed the car, and one of the mechanics that had been working on it said, Would you like to come back to my village? We'll have a feast, or barbecue, or words to that effect. This was after the car had been repaired. Our last night. And we said, Very nice. And he lived in a village called El Redal. He led the way from Logroño, on his scooter, we followed in the Mercedes. We'd left the caravan outside the garage where it had been worked on. It was quite a good road and then all of a sudden he turned off and we followed him for miles up this track. If we hadn't've known this place we would never have found it, not in a million years.

They stuck Mark up on a mule and took him all round the village. And there seemed to be hordes and hordes of people about. And nobody spoke English, we spoke no Spanish. And then they got the carcase of this sheep out and took us a little way up the hill, to the bodega, which is where they kept their wine, and I presume that this was a wine-growing village. In the bodega was this massive table, set out, I suppose enough places for about twenty-odd people, or more.

All in our honour, God knows why. They then took out a load of faggots, or bundles of what looked like pea-sticks, and cooked up this sheep's carcase. And the wine just kept coming, lots and lots of wine. And a lot of hilarity. For two groups of people who didn't speak each other's language it was amazing.

Then they sang and I asked them about their political affinities, and mentioned Franco, and a few of the younger ones, obviously a bit more headstrong, started making sort of noises, and I think a throat-cutting gesture was made, but the older members obviously cautioned them to keep the lid on it. I didn't know which way they were politically inclined, I didn't know an awful lot about the Spanish Civil War, but this place obviously was not sympathetic to Franco.

They entertained us royally. There were no other women there. There was Wendy and my mate's wife, and that was it, none of the woman from the village, which was rather odd. The men dished the food up and poured the wine. And kept pouring the wine, I mean we were bloody near legless by the time we'd finished. And this went on for quite a few hours and then we had to go. And I remember it was pitch dark, there were no lights there, and they took us by the hand, literally, to guide us back down to the village, which was only a few hundred yards away, but nevertheless down this steep sort of track from the bodega, back to the car.

Goodbye to Logroño   We got back to Logroño and the caravan and slept there OK for the night. And the next morning we drove back to say our proper farewells. And the whole village turned out, and the whole town as well. As we pulled out of Logroño the streets were lined with these people. And we'd obviously been friendly, it was not difficult to be friendly with people that are very friendly to you. And we said Goodbye, and we'd come back, and God knows what else, and we drove on.

We drove through the foothills of the Pyrenees, through Zaragosa, across to the Mediterranean coast, Barcelona and then on to a place where Brian had stayed previously with his parents on holiday, a place called Blanes, forty miles north of Barcelona.

This was a holiday town and had started to be exploited as a tourist place. A lot of Germans, a lot of hotels. And Brian obviously was very much at his ease there, he'd been there before, he knew where the bars were. I didn't like the place as much as I liked Logroño, despite the fact that the sea was there.

Spanish building site   My main concern was to get a job. So I hung around this building site for a couple of days, here and there, and asked people. Eventually I got a job on this site, building a hotel. The guy that actually got me the job was, I suppose some people would say, a real gypsy or dago-looking Spaniard, Andre Naranja Garban, which is Spanish for orange I think. I can always remember his name, but he was a very nice guy and got me the start. As a bricklayer, even though I'd never been a bricklayer in this country. I thought, Great, I'd heard all the rumours about the Spanish loafing about and all the rest of it. But I was in for a nasty shock, because I had to start at seven o'clock the next morning. So I thought I'd better get there early and make a good impression. But unlike here it's not, get on the job at seven o'clock, it's, you get on the job before seven o'clock. And you actually have to have the trowel in your hand ready to lay the first brick at seven o'clock, and that's spot-on, there's no messing about, a whistle goes and then *you start.*

The other guys were all friendly and there were one or two that were taking linguaphone courses in English so of course I was quite useful for them. I got one ticking-off from the foreman for not shouting at the boy that brought you the mortar or the water, when I said, Oh can I have some ... *por favor, agua* or whatever, he said, No, no, no, it's *Venga, venga.* Hurry up, hurry up. Well Christ, the kid's only about fourteen or fifteen if that. And then we stopped at one, I thought, Great, siesta. And it was one till half-past two siesta, but then it was half-past two to I think half-past eight at night. Again, working – you were busy.

My pay for a seventy-two hour week was the equivalent of four pound four, which was not a lot of money.

Reluctant return   Anyway at the end of that week it all fell apart. Brian said, We're going back to England. And Wendy was really, really upset. Badly upset. More upset than me I think.

And so in May 1962 we came back, via Perpignan. It was a bitter pill to swallow, because we'd only been gone a month. El Redal was the highlight. That was really nice, really nice. I shall never forget that.

Flat life   When we got back to England we had one and ninepence. Literally. And our share of what food was left over, which was maybe a dozen packets of dehydrated soup. Mark still wasn't two. We had to find somewhere to live, so we picked up the *Argus* straightaway of course – I'm still with Brian and the caravan's parked just outside Brighton – and we enquired after various flats. And then there was this flat in Whippingham Street. It was a house divided into two flats, with two separate entrances, so it was completely self-contained. And had two bedrooms, which was something we'd never had before, it was luxury. I got a job the next day virtually straightaway, working on a site for a guy that I'd worked for previously, a subcontractor, and everything was OK until the end of that first week, and then our troubles really began.

Harassment   The guy that owned the flat said, The one thing we do insist on, is that you pay the rent on time. Anyway the first Friday I got paid, and obviously Wendy and I had been living on bread and packet soup, for that week, so we'd done the shopping and we were late getting back to the flat. I thought, I'd better not knock him up now because he'll be up early if he's a milkman, I'll pay him tomorrow. Anyway I went to work the Saturday morning, came home and knocked on the door, and his wife – she was a Yugoslav – came down. I said, This is the rent, I didn't pay it last night because I didn't want to disturb your husband. So she just took it, gave me a funny look and took it, and then went in.

Half an hour later there was a knock on the door, and her husband was there, he said, Here's your rent back, he said, I want you out. I said, Why? He said, Because it was explained to you that I wanted the rent on time. I said, I explained to your wife, we had to do the shopping, we were late getting back last night, I didn't want to disturb you, so therefore I paid it today. I've been to work this morning. He said, I don't care. So I thought, Oh God, this is good isn't it. So anyway I took the rent, thought, Well that's it, we've got a month anyway.

So then maybe an hour or two later the wife came down, she wanted the money back and said, We'll let you off this time, it's OK, you can stay, it was just the heat of the moment. So I thought, Well that's all right, thank God for that, and we gave the money back.

But then virtually every day or every other day, there was some reason why they wanted to evict us, they wanted us out. You can stay, you can go, you can stay, you can go, and there were numerous rows. Wendy was pregnant again and things got to the point where it was so bad that her blood pressure was rising, and eventually she had to go into hospital with toxaemia.

I think that was one of the worst periods of our lives. Prior to going to hospital, every day Wendy was doing the rounds of the estate agents desperately trying to get us a place. She knew that if the harassment continued I would probably have done something that would have landed me inside. They were awful. No one should have that much power to make other people miserable, it was incredible. I'd got a job, I was bringing in a wage, we were paying our rent. And that was also the very bad winter of 1962-3. And quite a depressing place to live because that was on the way up to the churchyards and crematoria. There was an awful lot of funerals going on at that time. So that was a bad period, it built into me a real aversion for the Lewes Road area.

In the end we had to stay there for nine months, then we got an attic flat in Devonshire Place. I got hold of it through the Asian guy Hussein that I'd worked with, he was living in the basement and told me about this place. We moved on 2 February 1963. Wendy was eight months pregnant.

Attic flat   Stewart was born on 4 March 1963 and Wendy had to drag the pram up three floors. Which was not very convenient at all, and the flat was quite grotty. I think the previous tenant had worked on the railway, and left most of his railway grease on the furniture, because a lot of it was black and leather-looking, but it should have been like velvet. Anyway we were glad to get away from Whippingham Street. We moved in there and Wendy had Stewart and she was OK, and he was a very bonny baby. I think he was nine pounds.

We were OK there for about three months, then the ceiling in the lounge fell down because when the roof had been retiled the roofers had let a lot of the old slates and rubbish fall between the ceiling joists of our flat and not bothered to clear it. It was a one-bedroom flat and for x amount of weeks we virtually lived in the kitchenette and the bedroom. So I carried the ceiling and a load of old roof rubbish downstairs on my back in dustbins to get rid of it, and I got the plasterboard from a site, and got that up. The landlord didn't do much, although he was in fact a carpenter.

Bloody landlords   We'd been in that flat about a year when the landlord told us he was going to sell the house and wanted us out. The people that were coming in were buying it as a house to live in, with part of it to rent out. We had to be out of the top part. So I thought, My God, another bloody landlord. Obviously we started trying to look for a place, and we'd been on the Council list some time, but it was very difficult to find anywhere to live when you had children. When it was a single room or something like this, they seemed prepared to accept us, but if ever there was a flat that was halfway decent and had a garden or something, as soon as they found out you'd got children, they'd think up a hundred-and-one excuses as to why it wasn't suitable.

Then his brother who lived on the ground floor and was like the live-in caretaker of the flats, said to me, Well, you'll have to have your kids fostered till you get a place. And I said, Well quite honestly, and you can repeat this to your brother, I'll burn this house down before I do that, I'm not doing that, you can forget that.

So then the landlord came up with this bright idea. On the first floor someone had vacated one room and a kitchenette, and he offered me that. He said, I've consulted my solicitor, and if you refuse the alternative accommodation that I've offered, then any money I lose through not selling the house you will be liable for.

So in September 1964 we had to move down into this one room and a kitchenette, with two kids. Which was awful, I mean we were crowded enough up at the very top but this was even worse. But we had no alternative, we were still desperately trying to get a place.

Not a charity   That bad winter of 1962 to 1963 was one of the few times when I was off work for a while. The first couple of weeks it's not too bad, you've got no heavy bills coming, but then after a bit, bills mount up, especially when the children are very young. They don't wear things out, they grow out of them.

We were finished up on the Friday, go up to Upper North Street to sign on, then go from Upper North Street to the Social Security, which was in Ship Street I think at that time. You join a queue there, then when you get to the counter, they say, Where's Form B31? or something like that, have you got that? No. Well, don't come here till you've got that, you should have got that at the

Labour Exchange. So you then go back up to Upper North Street, get Form B31, whatever, by this time it's lunchtime and they've shut the office at Ship Street. You go back and join the queue at Ship Street with your B31 form, get in the queue there again, which obviously you've lost your previous place. You then get to the counter and they say, Where do you live? And you say, I live So-and-So, So-and-So, they say, Oh no, you've got to go to the St James Street branch. And then when you get up to the St James Street branch, again you're at the back of a queue. So this is stressful, believe you me.

Well, when I actually got in, the amount of money they'd paid me didn't even cover my rent, and at that time if you didn't pay the rent on time, you could be evicted by your landlord, a private landlord, no problem. And I threw the money back, I couldn't throw it at his face, but I threw it back at him under the glass partition, and I said, That's not enough, it doesn't even pay my rent. And his reply was, This is not a charity, we're not supposed to pay your rent, you know. I said, I know it's not a charity, I said, because I and all those guys out there are paying for this, and your wages every week, Mister. Now what is this?

We survived, we did, we did survive, obviously. But that business of being shunted from one office to the other, I don't know if it's a ploy or just a bad system, or what the system is now, but it certainly was very demoralising. Very demoralising. We weren't scroungers, we were out of work because of the weather.

That particular bad winter there were thousands of building workers in the Brighton area off work because of the weather, and the DHSS called me in after a couple of weeks and told me my money was going to be cut by two pound a week. And this was extremely stressful.

Fraught   It was quite a nightmare really, Devonshire Place, oh yes. Can't remember many good things about it at all. We'd have rows. Quite a lot. Sometimes we disagreed over parenting, I think the same thing happens with a lot of couples. Wendy's spontaneous, she will rant and rave, and she goes off quick. Whereas, I mean I can get annoyed, but I'm far more cold-blooded. And if I was going to punish the kids for something, she'd instinctively protect them, and this would lead to a row, because if I'm determined to do something, be it reprimand them or smack them, whatever, I'm going to do it. And all she does by interfering is escalate an already fraught situation, she won't stop me chastising them.

If you don't have an immediately all-embracing family, and you don't have money, you just have to tolerate an awful lot of things that if you were slightly better off, or slightly better situated, you wouldn't tolerate. That's the situation we were in. We didn't have anywhere to go, literally.

I couldn't have just moved into digs. Well I could, some guys did, one week there'd be a wage coming in, the next week there wouldn't, they'd just buggered off somewhere, they'd get digs or a room with somebody else. I could never do that. I was always very aware of what my responsibilities were. I mean, you know, we'd created this family or this situation, so, we had to get on with it. It's as simple as that.

The new owners subsequently moved in, and they were a nice couple and it turned out in actual fact that they hadn't wanted the top part vacant at all, so this was an absolute nonsense. But work had started to be done on the top flat, which as I say was pretty grotty anyway, so we had to stay where we were for another few months.

Part Two:
Life in the Trenches

INTO THE TRENCHES

Irish gang   In 1964 I started a new chapter in my life. A friend of mine, an Irish guy called Brian O'Connor that I'd worked with for Evershed, asked me if I fancied going on piecework. He said the crack would be good. So I said yes. And I started working with him on this all-Irish pipe-laying gang, there was four or five of us. From now on until 1990 I'd be working for a succession of firms who had the Sussex contract to lay pipes for British Gas, later Transco.

We were digging the trenches on a sub-contract for O. C. Summers, or OCS. We weren't direct employees, I was taken on by a subcontractor, and he paid me x amount a week. We were working in a place called Forest Row, which is near East Grinstead. And it was a good crack. The work was damn hard, I mean I didn't think I'd stick it, because of the pace they were working at. But everybody was helpful, and I think they made allowances, but not obviously so, for my lack of experience and ability to keep up.

We used to have the most enormous fry-ups every morning, that was fantastic. It was in the winter when I started and I used to get stuck into black pudding, which I'd never liked before, bacon, eggs, at least half a small loaf of bread and quarter of a pound of butter, and a pint of milk, every morning, without fail. And then a smaller version of that at lunchtime as well.

And the lads were good. I mean when we couldn't get on for some reason or the other we used to play hurley with pick handles. It was my introduction to hurley and it's no mean thing to be confronted by six foot four of West of Ireland lunatic coming at you swinging a pick handle round his head. I'm sure that's not part of the proper rules of hurley but nevertheless. You do have a ball, they call it the shlitter. And there's apparently an awful lot of head injuries, which I'm not surprised at. And on most occasions I found that discretion was the better part of valour and I used to get out of their way. But it was fun and it sort of cemented your get-together as a crew. We were up there I suppose for about a month.

Five shillings a yard   The gang then came down and started work at Haywards Heath, for a firm called McCullough's, that then had the Sussex contract. But the arrangement was different then, because it was piecework, through another subcontractor called Michael Hilary, a Clare man. We had to do it on a yardage price, and the price at that time was five shillings a linear yard. That's digging it out at least three foot deep, and as narrow as we could get the pipe in, and backfilling, that means filling in the trench afterwards. And that was for five shillings. And that was hard work, that was very hard.

Also, obviously after you've displaced x amount of soil, the soil left over used to be loaded onto a tipper lorry. We didn't have those hydraulic grabs that you see now, we had to load it on by hand and we each used to get half a crown a cubic yard, for loading that. And shovelling it off of grass, wet clay, was an awful job, but it was part of the job and we just had to do it.

Tearing into it   There was a certain amount of competition as regards the job, inasmuch that if you didn't cut it as a pieceworker, your partner, or partners – sometimes there were three or four of us – wouldn't carry you, or couldn't carry you. So you had to keep your end up even if you weren't feeling too good. There were one or two times when blokes were carried, I remember one guy that had his hand in plaster, and he shouldn't have been at work at all, but we carried him for a couple of weeks. But he would do more than keep his end up in normal times. He was an English guy called Jimmy McKechnie. He'd got his hand in plaster because he'd punched his wife in the head and broken his fist. A little guy.

It was important to prove to myself that I could do it, and I wouldn't be beaten by adverse conditions or whatever. If somebody could dig out eight yards and I could only dig out six, I wouldn't think I had got to beat that, as long as that six was my maximum effort, that's how I felt. I would do the best that I could with what I'd got, as it were. It's pushing myself but it's not being competitive. I compete against myself if you like.

Mr Freely was the first to suggest I had an aggressive attitude to work. I suppose it's true. If I was given something physical to do, and most of my work in life has been an awful lot of hard physical work, I would virtually have to get my blood up to do it. There have been lots of situations where I was really tired, didn't want to do anything, and would have sat down if I'd had any choice, but instead of that I would get what I would call my second wind and really attack what I was doing.

I don't actually think Freely had seen me at my most aggressive. It was more later, when I was a pieceworker, navvying, that I would almost have to psyche myself up to tear into it. Possibly because in that line of business I didn't rate as being really tough compared with an awful lot of those people I worked with, for example my long-standing mate Dan, because I know that I'm not physically as strong as him, although I know I am physically strong compared to the average person of my age, or even younger.

People don't appreciate how strong, tough and resilient a lot of these men are that did this sort of job. There aren't many like them around today. Quite a few of them are dead, maybe because they burned themselves out when they were quite young. Also the job is more mechanised, there's less need for hard physical labour.

Better out than in   As a pieceworker you just had to be aggressive to get stuck in, because it was hard. And even if you were on ground that was softer, and easier to dig, then you just expected yourself to do twice as much. Also when it was hot, and it does get hot in this country, especially if you're digging, you had to really push yourself. And if it's wet you have to push yourself even more.

I think wet is the worst thing, worse than cold or heat, because everything you touch is sticky and slimy and you get covered up to your hips. I think an awful lot of guys that have worked in trenches end up having hip trouble, and bad rheumatism, because when you're a pieceworker you dig the trench as narrow as you can get away with. But it has to be three foot deep or in some cases deeper if there were obstacles. So therefore your hips are constantly wet, even in summertime. Quite often where the water table is high, up round say Haywards Heath and Burgess Hill, the clay is wet, once you break the surface out.

At the same time, you know the alternative is to do one of those other jobs, either in an office or a factory, and you know you couldn't do it. I've tried, I have worked a couple of times indoors, in the worst of weather, the worst time of the year, and I couldn't stick it, I didn't like it. So it's the lesser of the two evils. That may seem illogical to people that can't see the sense in going out and getting cold and wet all day, but that's just the way I am and a lot of men are the same. A lot of men are the same.

Another aspect, it may sound contradictory, but there's a freedom about it. I don't have to go to work and be nice to people.

Piecework & daywork Formally I was a self-employed pieceworker. Piecework is a really bad system. Some jobs you can cut corners, and I know guys that do, but when you're actually digging and it's measured work, and the person that is measuring and assessing what you've done is not affected by what you get, it's not like a chain where everybody links together. The gangerman was indifferent as to whether you got five yards out or fifty yards out, he wanted it dug a certain depth and that was it. So you couldn't make any short cuts there.

And if it took you longer to do the yardage, him and the jointer and the pipelayer had less work to do, they hadn't got as many pipes to lay. On some of the gangs, the ganger and the jointer would sit in the shed all day, and do nothing. Now when I became a ganger, later on, I never ever did that, never sat in the shed while the other lads were out there digging, I mean I just couldn't do it. Even if I didn't dig in with them I'd find something else to do. I regarded it as a team, and I couldn't stand by and watch other people working.

But the iniquitous thing about the system was when you got what they called daywork. If for example the jointer and the ganger and the pipelayer were making a connection, and there wasn't really a lot the pieceworkers could do, apart from hand down tools to them, sweep up or whatever, you were paid so much a day. Now if you did a full week of this daywork, which we would call scratching about, you would get four pound a day. If you did four days daywork and one day piecework, then the money for the daywork rate was cut down to three pound five. The theory was that you could make up the money in piecework, but obviously you can't. I never agreed with that, but that was the terms of the job and you had to accept it. It was a little wrinkle, a stroke the subbie used to pull.

Gangers! I think in the early days the ganger used to get backhanders from the subbie, for using the subbie's labour, and for trying to work as much stuff as he could with the pencil when booking the work in. He would book maybe extra depth or things he could get away with. Some of the gangermen I worked for, and one in particular, if they did anything at all to help you, like take a little bit out of the bottom of the trench because you hadn't taken it quite deep enough, or shovel a bit of dirt back in on top of the pipe, they would have their hand out at the end of the week for a couple of quid. And you had to cough up.

In those days, not all these companies had vans. Invariably the gangermen would have a car, and they did get a car allowance, so much for running the car and putting petrol in it. It depended on the gangerman, as to whether or not they would give the piece-workers a lift. Some would, some wouldn't.

One job, there was this vast estate out at Eastbourne, and I was given the line where I'd got to dig, and for two days I've got maybe two thousand yards in front of me, or more than that. And the ganger and jointer, apart from going to the café, sat in his car and watched me. Which I didn't like at all. I didn't mind if they bug-gered off, but when you can't even see the horizon on the job as it were, to think you've got to do that all on your own, with these two monkeys sitting in a car watching you, it wasn't good. Plus the fact that he didn't take me to the café, and he had his hand over the back seat the first day and said he wanted money for driving me out to the job. Even though they were getting their petrol allowance from the firm.

So I went back to the subbie on the Sunday, met him in the pub, I said, I'm not going out with Clancy any more, I'm not going to have someone sit watching me digging away on my own like an idiot. So he's then sent me out back up with this other ganger.

Another time, we were working at Slindon, near Arundel, but we had to get a train from Brighton to Barnham, and then walk from Barnham Station to this job. It must have been three or four miles. And the particular ganger I was working with would never, ever, give us a lift. He took his jointer in his car, he was a drinking mate, but no matter how bad the day had been, how wet it was, he would never give us a lift. The day I had an accident to my finger he wouldn't even take me to hospital. And both of them, if we were just digging, and the ground was hard there, so there wouldn't be a lot of pipes going in, they would sit for two or three days doing absolutely nothing.

Disposable   There was a very rigid hierarchy between the direct employed and the pieceworkers. We were just disposable, like a bit of scrap paper that could be picked up or thrown away whenever they felt like it. And if the ganger said he didn't want you, if you fell out with him, then you went, there was no question of arguing or asking for notice or anything like that. I've seen guys sacked on the spot loads of times. I've never been sacked on the spot. I did have a row with one ganger, but that was after I became employed.

There was no basic wage, and I had no guarantee whatsoever. I mean theoretically if it rained five days, and we literally couldn't get out and do it, although we did often work in the rain, you didn't get paid. Even though you were there. I always used the argument that, irrespective of whether I'm doing something or not, it's my time when I'm somewhere where I don't want to be, I should be paid for it. But that sort of argument didn't cut any ice. Sometimes when I was asked to work overtime I would refuse. When it was pointed out to me how much extra I would earn I'd reply, You can't buy back time once it has gone. I don't think they understood this concept.

Subbies   If you wanted a job you would go to a particular pub on a Sunday, which was the sort of unofficial labour exchange for that particular subbie. The Cliftonville was where we used to go, which is the pub just down from Hove Station, it's under a different name now. We'd go in there and say, Any chance of a start? And he would either give you the start or not. And once you sort of knew people in the trade, you'd get to hear about where jobs were. This was what you did, but you didn't go to the company and ask to get a job or anything like that.

There'd invariably only be one subbie in the pub. That would be his particular patch, and other subbies would recruit in other pubs, for the most part. The Cliftonville was mixed English and Irish but there were various pubs that were called Irish pubs, because a lot of Irish used to frequent them. Like the Railway, up by Brighton station, that was nearly all Irish because there was a lot of lodging houses and stuff round there, and bedsits of a very humble variety, so that was a natural area for the Irish to be in.

The subbies would draw from the company the money that you'd earned and take their percentage out, I never knew exactly what it was. They did nothing, they laid out *nothing*. They didn't buy any tools, they didn't buy any clothes, they didn't pay for your stamps. They were parasitic.

The pieceworkers didn't go in the pub to get paid, no, they'd go in there for a sub maybe, on the Sunday, when they were skint. They would either go to a collection point, on Thursdays, to be paid by the subbies, or sometimes the subcontractors would bring the money round. These collecting points would be Brighton Station, the Seven Dials, and Preston Circus. If you ask anybody that's lived in those areas for twenty or thirty years, they will remember the great gatherings of lorries and vans of various contractors at these points on a Thursday morning. You might get six or seven vans up round the Seven Dials or whatever. They parked their vans, then the pieceworkers would walk down to the subbie, who'd be standing in a shop doorway or sitting in his car, passing out the money. You'd also be picked up from these collecting points to go to work.

And there's the popular picture of the subcontractor pulling up on the job on the Thursday, sitting in his car with the engine running and the car in gear, wind down the window half an inch, pass out two brown envelopes and bugger off quick. I didn't see that happen but there was one occasion when two Irish guys thought they'd been done out of some money, and they proceeded to throw the contents of the washing-up bucket all over the subbie and to hold him to ransom with an iron pin till he paid out what they thought they were owed. And another subbie was knocked down on the road and one of those very heavy rammers was bounced to and fro across his head, both sides of his head, bouncing to and fro. Those very heavy things, you don't see them on the roads now, used to call them jumping jacks. And he had a nervous breakdown, we never saw him again. That was because they thought they'd been robbed.

I'm not so sure that it's totally finished, but I haven't had any connection with that sort of thing for many many years. When I was a ganger, initially, I did have, on some of the firms, a few guys that worked for subcontractors. But it's stopped now. Everybody has to be on the cards, regular.

Joe the Butcher   After the Irish gang split up I went to work with an English guy, an English ganger, still on piecework, out at

Slindon. And I was working with an Irish guy whose nickname was Joe the Butcher, because that had been his trade. Quite appropriate as it turned out.

We were hand-digging and it was horrible ground. It's very important to a pieceworker what the ground's like, digging in one place is very different than digging in another. And this ground was mixed clay and gravel, very hard ground, with lots of flint in it. You couldn't use what we call a grafter, which is a tapered shovel whereby you could cut out pieces weighing forty-odd pound to throw out the trench at a time, and make quite a neat job of it. And we didn't have a compressor there, so there was no pneumatic drill.

So I was breaking this very hard ground down to him with a fork, which is quite a heavy tool because it's iron all the way up to the handle. And because the ground was so hard I was having to use an awful lot of force to bring the fork down.

And he had an awful habit of waiting with the shovel slanting up, like when you hold a rifle up, almost in the on guard position, while I was cutting down. I'd warned him loads of times not to stand like that, or if he insisted, to stand further back. But this particular time Joe has done his usual nonsense of leaning in towards me, not paying attention to what was going on. And as I've come down with the fork, bashing downwards, very hard, I've met the blade of the shovel with my fingers, that are gripped very tightly round the fork handle.

And I just shook my hand, and said, You prat Joe, I said, I've effing well told you about that, for Christ's sake. And put my hand back down and started to continue digging. And then a couple of minutes later he said, Jesus Christ, look at the fork.

Out cold   And when I looked down the whole handle of the fork right down to the tines was absolutely red, it was just covered in blood. I said, Oh Jesus, and I held my hand up with my fingers horizontal, but the end of the middle finger on my right hand just flopped and hung there by what looked like a little bit of skin. I thought, Oh Christ he's really done it this time.

And then I looked up to see Joe, and Joe wasn't where he should have been, Joe was horizontal back in the trench, he'd passed out. Which even though I was in a great deal of pain at the time I thought was hilarious. And the other finger beside it was cut quite badly as well, but not to that extent.

Stitched up   So anyway I've climbed out the trench and I've said to the ganger, I've got to go to hospital with this Bert, I've got to get this seen to. And he said in his gruff voice, Well you'll have to wait till the compressor comes back. This was the mobile compressor, which was mounted on a lorry. That'll be back in a minute, he said, he'll take you. Now Bert had a car on the job at the time. But he wouldn't take me in his car to the hospital. He didn't want blood and stuff in his car, not that it would have been, I'd have wrapped a rag or my shirt round it. So I waited about twenty minutes, half an hour. The mobile compressor came back and he grudgingly gave the driver permission to drive me to the hospital.

I was on the operating table for about an hour and a half with them trying to stick my finger together. When I came out of there it was all stitched up, bound up, with a steel splint.

I eventually got out of the hospital, Christ, it was about nine o'clock that evening, and I hadn't got any money to get home with. And one of the nurses gave me some sandwiches and I think the almoner gave me some money. I had my arm in a sling and all the rest of it. I got home about ten, half-past ten that night. Wendy had wondered what the hell had happened, she didn't know, no one had been to see her. The gangerman lived in Worthing, there was no way he would have driven over to Brighton, even if he knew where I lived. That was at Devonshire Place. We weren't on the phone.

Claw   Anyway so that was that, and I was off work I think for six weeks. But then because we were getting in dire straits as far as money was concerned, I had to go back to work, so it meant the steel splint had to come off, because obviously when you have to grip things, you can't have your finger stuck out at right angles to your hand. Which is why the finger is bent to this day. If I'd managed to do the full term off sick, with the finger kept absolutely rigidly straight, then it might have healed properly and I don't think I would have the unsightly finger that I've got now. Which is a standing joke amongst my friends, about it being a claw or looking like a tree-root. Whenever I cut myself, Dan'll say, Oh another bit of bark off the limb.

I can't straighten it, I just can't. It's bent forward and it's bent to the left. The only time it's a problem is if I'm sandpapering anything, it tends to curl underneath and get jammed under the sandpaper, or the block. Apart from that I'll never play the piano again, but then I never could anyway. And I can give a particularly obscene version of the finger signal to people.

Good team   Anyway I went back to work with my bent finger, back to the piecework, and by this time my mate Dan was working with me, and we were a good team, we could get through an awful lot of work. That first year he worked with me, we figured out that for the whole year we'd been stripped to the waist every week, even in January, February and March. I can quite clearly remember carrying steel pipes with snow on them on our bare shoulders and how cold it felt. We were working that hard. That was busy.

I did earn good money on one job, at Hassocks. Two of us dug out eighty yards of sand in a day. It was a bit like damp sand you get on some beaches, it didn't collapse straight away, it was unique, you could just dig it with a shovel. That was about the best we ever did.

But it was not work for a lot of money, it was work to make a wage. There's no way we'd have got rich.

New Steine, new life   Then we moved down to New Steine, off the sea-front in Kemp Town, almost next door to Devonshire Place. This would have been 1965. This was a basement flat, with no one below us. The landlord lived on the top floor with his wife and there were some older tenants above us but we didn't have to worry about the kids running about and disturbing people and it was quite a nice flat in fact. We were still on the Council list, and approached them from time to time: still nothing, we hadn't got enough points, whatever. In fact I think we're still on the bloody Council list to this day, because we've never asked for our names to be retracted.

Good times   New Steine was a good flat. It was only one bedroom, but it was quite a large one, then we had a large lounge, a small kitchen and a bathroom with a toilet. It was totally self-contained and we had a small back yard and an entrance onto another street.

The kids slept in the bedroom and had all their stuff in there. We had wardrobes in there, but we had to sleep on the put-you-up.

The old couple upstairs and their son were friends of ours. It was quite funny, Wendy would hear a tap on the window and there'd be a toothbrush on a bit of string coming down, tapping on the kitchen window. He'd shout, Wen, send us some tooth-paste if you've got any to spare will you? That was quite nice, that was nice.

We stayed there eleven years. It was our first proper family home, we put down some roots and met most of our friends there.

You had the grass in the little square out at the front, which was handy because the kids used to go up there and throw balls around, and run about. The hazard of course was that an awful lot of people used it as a dog-toilet. One particular guy round the corner had two Great Danes that he kept in his flat, and he would bring them out onto the grass twice a day. One of my friends in an idle moment worked out how many pounds of dog excreta there could have been on that bit of grass from those two alone. But apart from that it was OK.

A sixties group   We'd lots of friends who used to come down and we became part of a sort of group which met round the corner at the Royal Oak in St James Street. Nothing special about the Oak except we went there, we made it like our own.

They were mixed. Antonia was obviously from a middle-class background, Tony B went to art college. There was a few that were involved in the art world, mainly from Croydon Art College, that had moved down here. The new landlord of Devonshire Place was George Popplewell who taught there, but the main influence was Clifford Frith who was Principal of Fine Art. He would come down to New Steine or we would go to his place, he had a house along the front. There was Fred Carver who I suppose was near-est to being working-class but he was also lecturing at Croydon, from being a student there. And his lady. Some were dropouts from College, or just didn't want to work. Hippies.

There was the guy I shared a boat with, Alan, he was a tool-maker, or that's what he started off as, but he became something in engineering, quite a clever guy. And his wife, Ruth, who was a model, quite an outstanding lady one way and another. They were there a lot. I think none of the other people apart from Alan and

10. Stag weekend in the New Forest, about 1963. Peter in the middle, Dan seated next to him on the right, and Lou, another old mate, sitting on the left.

Ruth had any children, so we couldn't go out as much but they'd tend to come to us.

I don't think there was anybody else from my type of work except Dan, he mixed in quite well but not that often. I was the odd one out I suppose really. I don't remember having any difficulty in keeping up with them, whatever we were discussing. Because I read a lot then, and had read a lot previously. And my life's experiences were different I suppose from most manual workers.

So we had lots of people coming round, especially after the pubs shut. Sometimes Wendy would be preparing enough bacon sandwiches for maybe fourteen or fifteen people. It was very sociable. When people came to stay it was pretty cramped, that was incredible, it was like a flop-house. And the fact that we had kids didn't seem to cramp our social life at all, we started going to quite a lot of parties at that time. This was the start of the sort of hippy era, and we'd take the kids with us.

Part-time hippy It got to be a bit of a drag sometimes as it was quite the fashion then to drop out, and people would stay rather late, and I had to get up for work early, and as the put-you-up couldn't be put up until they'd gone, I sometimes didn't get to bed as early as I'd like to. People that are not working the next day quite like sitting around to two o'clock in the morning listening to Pink Floyd and whatever. I used to say I was only a part-time hippy, but again I never really fell out with anybody over that. So it was nice, we had lots of fun, lots of friends, it was a good time.

At first we didn't have a great deal of money, but from about 1970 I did start to earn a lot more because natural gas was coming through and I was working sometimes seven days, and we'd do a couple of nights. So my money was quite good at the time and we could afford luxuries like going to pop concerts and things, as well as parties. It was quite good.

Space share Stefan was born in 1967 when we'd been a couple of years at New Steine. He was really indulged, he was a really nice baby, a very pretty baby. People liked him, he'd a nice sort of personality, which he still has. But Keith, the guy that lived upstairs, was a so-and-so, he used to come in from the pub and insist on getting Stefan up, because he loved him. Then he would always go up to bed at midnight, he was like bloody Cinderella, but we had the problem of getting Stefan back to sleep, every night.

But the thing about living in that sort of cramped accommodation is you can *not* be too self-indulgent, you can't slam off into another room, you can't be terribly anti-social, it just doesn't allow it. Which is why I think we tend to be quite sort of tolerant with each other.

Late home   It wasn't all sweetness and light. There were two incidents when things turned nasty, or I turned nasty. Nothing to do with the conditions we were living in, it would have been the same if we were living in a five-bedroomed house.

The first time was not long after we'd moved to New Steine.

It was all over nothing really. Alan and I used to go to the Royal Oak, just up the road. On this particular occasion, we said we'd go and play bar billiards but we wouldn't be all that long. His wife Ruth was at our place, I think they were staying the weekend. And anyway some other friends rolled up, two women, Marina and Lynn. And we played bar billiards with them. And we were there a bit longer than we expected to be.

Anyway we came back down to New Steine, and Wendy was absolutely furious. I suppose we were about an hour later than we'd said. She said, You told me you weren't going to be long. I said, All right, I'm sorry ... She said, Oh it's just because Lynn and Marina were up there. I said OK ... And Wendy just kept on. I said, Now, all right, I'm in the wrong, I didn't stay up there just because there was two women there, we were playing bar billiards, lost track of the time, that's it. And Wendy still wouldn't leave it, she wouldn't stop going on about it, You told me ..., it was just because those women were up there, that's why you stayed up there, you don't care about us, and blah blah, it went on and on.

Domestic violence   I said, Now shut up, I've had enough, pack it up, I've said I was in the wrong, or I've said I'm sorry, whatever, you won't leave it alone will you? And again, No I'm not going to leave it alone ... and then I just jumped across the kitchen and head-butted her in the face. I don't know if it was once or twice that I did it. But I mean usually when I've done that once it's been enough for anybody. And that was it.

I don't know if I would have reacted as strongly if there hadn't been an audience, but it was almost like a contest. And I was not going to lose, or crack first. I did give Wendy the opportunity to back off, well not back off, but stop going on about it. But she didn't stop.

I think the violence kicks in when I feel there are no more words to express what I'm feeling. It's when the words run out, yes. Or, you think the words are not getting home.

Pent up   The second time was entirely different. Wendy had gone over to see friends in a house near Brighton Station, you could say it was almost a commune-type place. This would be middle seventies. And it was a weekday, so eleven would have been about as late as I would have expected her back. Anyway time went on, I think it got to be one o'clock. I know it's only two hours after, but I really started to get in a state, wondering and worrying. I've got a very fertile imagination when it comes to worrying. All sorts of accidents, kidnappings, assault, whatever. Because that area can be quite dodgy at night, with various undesirables that live and hang around there. So eventually, the kids were asleep, so I went over to this house, keeping my eyes open all the time on the way to see if there was any signs of any accident or whatever. And Wendy was sitting on this sofa, beside this guy that I knew, little guy.

And she said, I didn't realise how late it was or something like that. I mean I can see in my mind, I can see the picture of her sitting beside this other little guy. As clear as anything. Just sitting there. He was a heroin addict, but that's just by-the-by. I didn't think of any sort of adultery, anything like that. And, What the fuck, where, what is your fucking game? I've been worrying myself fucking sick, what the fuck do you think this is? And that's when she stood up, and bang, I was so pent up I just lashed out, lashed out a few times, quite a few times. It wasn't relief I felt, it wasn't relief at all, it was just the opposite, I think I just went up to another step of emotions. Nobody tried to interfere, they were too scared, yes. And I sort of dragged her out of the house. And the verbal went on all the way home.

Hand-grenade   It just felt like a spring had suddenly been uncoiled. Suddenly. That's what the feeling was. That's it, it's just boom, and it goes. It's like that.

Or, it's like a hand-grenade. The pin was in until I got closer to the house where she was. The closer I got, the less evidence there was of something happening, but the nearer I got I'm seething more and more, I've come more to the boil. This is the illogical part of it, the less reason there is to be worried, the madder I got.

So that's when, if you like, the pin was pulled, when I got in the house. But the handle is being held. And then when I get upstairs, it's all quite calm, there's nothing, she's just sitting there.

11. *Wendy and the children – Stewart, Stefan, and Mark – on Brighton Beach.*

That's it. I've been in all this state, she's flat calm. I've been getting myself in that state for absolutely no reason at all, it's cost me God knows what as far as stress or whatever. Obviously you don't think in those terms at the time, but it's been gnawing at you and hurting you inside, oh God yes, very much so.

The next day, I was working very close to Brighton Station somewhere, and Wendy came up, with a friend, to see me on the site where I was working, and her face did look quite a mess. Lips all broken and swollen, nose very swollen, a lot of bruising round the face. Maybe to show me in broad daylight what damage I'd done, I don't know.

Retrospect   I didn't feel sorry, that day. I didn't regret it. Later on, I did regret it, to a degree.

But years later, she told me she'd been having a one-night fling with this other guy that lived in the house. I think it was when she thought it was long enough after, and he'd gone away. We can talk about things that happened in the past, now, where we don't react, time has knocked the corners off as it were. Anyway, when I found out, I felt a little bit easier with my conscience, about the action that I took.

Nasty   But at the time the other people in the house had taken great pains to hide him somewhere where I wouldn't see him. Everybody knew what I was like and knew my reputation. They all thought, and a lot of it is myth, I was some sort of hard case and could be very nasty.

Well I can be very nasty, I know that, I know I'm very dangerous, inasmuch that I don't go into a blind rage. My sort of rage is cold but nevertheless it is as powerful as a red-hot rage I think. I feel it's more dangerous than someone who just goes berserk. I wasn't doing it blindly, I was picking where I was hitting. I even think about the consequences as I'm doing it. I do know that if I am crossed badly, I mean really seriously, I am very nasty. But I think most people have got that in them anyway.

Anxiety and anger   It was almost like another situation, years later, when I whacked Mark when the three boys went fishing at night from the harbour arm. I was getting in a terrible state, I was getting very frightened that they'd be swept off the arm and end up ... And then I met them calmly coming home, walking up the road, half-past twelve, one o'clock in the morning. And, Whack!

I can see it's a paradox, yes. I've told Dan about this, he says, You're the only fucking lunatic I know that gets really worried about someone getting hurt and then comes along and goes bang and does it.

Unfinished business   It's funny – funny's not the word – I don't feel ashamed.

But the real thing that still sticks in my craw even now is that I never got my hands on that bastard. I'd have hospitalised him, no doubt about it. And I probably wouldn't have attacked Wendy, no, I would have concentrated on him.

There's a retrospective anger, yes, and it's very powerful. The same as I felt about Fred maybe, but he's gone into the background. But with that particular guy it still feels like unfinished business.

I do believe in the vendetta. I have got that nasty streak even though 99.9 per cent of the time it is under control.

One of the few things in my life, when I did feel bitterly ashamed, is when I had a ruck in the cinema with a group of barrow boys, and I backed off. And I felt so humiliated after that.

The film was called *The Gazebo*. And there's one sitting the other side of Wendy who was using a lot of language, loudly, all the time, it was Sunday afternoon. So I said, Can you mind your language a bit, eh? And then he looks behind him and seeing he's getting the approbation of the other lot behind him, who I didn't realise were there, he said, What you going to do if I don't, what you going to fucking do if I don't? I said, I'll shove the words back down your throat. And then this lot behind me stood up, about four of them, Oh yeah, well come on then.

I thought, Well what shall I do. I could do him, get one or two belts in, do him quickly, but I know I'm going to get it. So I duly just got up and walked out. And to this day I regret really not banging the hell out of that one herbert, getting a few digs in first.

I do feel ashamed of walking out, and backing off.

But I don't feel ashamed about attacking Wendy for staying late, no. No.

Shit happens   Up until reasonably modern times people believed it was a man's right, if not his duty, to beat his wife up now and then. In some households Friday night violence was almost a ritual. I never subscribed to that. It is not acceptable that a man should hit his partner, in fact I don't believe I have a right to use violence against anybody. It's just something that happens. I regret it, but I don't feel ashamed. Shit happens. You don't want it to, but it happens.

A bit of a hiss   When I was working with another Irish gang as a pieceworker, someone got the idea, an engineer, that all of a sudden we should paint the nuts and bolts with synthaprufe, so they would not corrode. These were the nuts and bolts that held the joints together, they were spigot socket joints with a flange. They get these brainstorms now and again, after three or four weeks they'll forget it, and not bother. Anyway this guy insisted we do it.

Somebody had left the lid off this synthaprufe, so to use it we had to put it on our coke brazier, which we all used to carry in those days, and get it melted. And the ganger told me to paint these nuts and bolts with this stuff. So I got this synthaprufe molten, and I was standing on this pipe, it was quite wet and muddy on this job. And I'd painted one set of bolts, I was well down in the trench, and I turned round with the tin in one hand, the brush in the other, to paint the others, and my foot slipped off the pipe. Consequently my hands went up in the air and the tin of boiling synthaprufe, still bubbling, went over my left hand. Completely covered my left hand.

I'll always remember to this day, it even gave off a bit of a hiss when it hit my hand. And I shook my hand, Oh Christ that hurt. And I, funnily enough I carried on, I didn't react, except that I thought, Oh God, I'm going to have a job to get this stuff off. But then after about ten minutes the pain started coming on, and pain like I've never experienced before, it was incredible. When my finger was severed it hurt, but compared to burning with the synthaprufe it was nothing.

Headbanging So I've got out of the trench, and the gangerman was there, this Irish guy, and I said, Mick, I said, I can't put up with this, I've got to go home.

He didn't offer to drive me home – we were working in Burgess Hill at this time – so I had to run up to the station, get on the train and come home. All the time the pain was increasing and the hands were swelling, swelling to the extent that my fingers were getting bigger and bigger, they looked like black bananas. And all the time I was on the train, and the train was moving, I held my hand out of the window, it eased the pain a lot. I got to Brighton and got out of the station, and the pain came back on, and I just couldn't stand still long enough to get on the bus, so I ran home from the station, ran up to New Steine, and when I got home I said, Wendy, go up the chemist's for Christ's sake and get me something for these burns, because, you know, this pain was incredible. Wendy says that when she came back I was out the back bashing my head against the doorpost, it was hurting that much. And she said, The chemist said you'd better go up the hospital.

By this time, although my hand was spread wide out, the fingers were touching, the blisters were that bad. So I don't know if

I got a bus or I ran up to the Sussex County, and was taken straight in there. With burns they don't mess you around, you don't have a long wait, they take you in and deal with you straightaway because apparently there's some sort of shock. But this was about two-and-a-half hours or so after I'd actually had the accident.

They left the tar on, I don't know if it was because it was acting like some sort of antiseptic, but they didn't try and take it off. They gave me pain-killers and that night was quite painful but after that it eased off.

I was off work for about five or six weeks. Didn't get paid of course, got whatever the government paid at that time, which was a pittance.

I suppose people will gather from these two incidents, both the burning and having the finger chopped off, that the gangers were pretty callous. And they were.

Water bomb Another thing had happened when I was still a pieceworker for McCullough's, I was lucky there.

I was pulling brick rubble out from the bottom of the trench, literally just seeing a brick and pulling it with a pick, to get it out of the sand. All of a sudden, I thought I'd hit a bomb or a grenade, there was an explosion. And what it was, there'd been a plastic water-main laid there, and it was under pressure, and because of all the stuff that had gone on top it was like a balloon that had been squeezed, and just touching it with a pick, it exploded. It went off with a hell of a bang and it blew the glass out of my glasses. And my mate who was about ten, twelve feet away, half a brick hit him on the back of the head. It didn't do any serious damage, but I mean that's the extent of the explosion. I was OK, it did my glasses in. But when the agent for the company heard about this he said, Oh sack him, he's accident-prone. That was the reaction, yeah, that was the reaction. Funny thing was he was sacked himself a few weeks later.

But the subbie that I worked for, he didn't sack me, in fact he gave me a couple of quid for some new glasses. I think it frightened him quite honestly.

Hierarchy In the gang you normally used to have at least two pieceworkers. The pieceworkers did the digging, backfilling, and any really heavy humping, or had to muck in. Sometimes it was four, depending on what size work was being done, the diameter and length of the job, but usually two. It's only the piece-workers who were on subcontract, the subcontractors were just providing labour for the contractor. As I say, we were a very easily disposable labour force. You could be hired and fired at a minute's notice like that.

Then there was a pipelayer, a jointer and the ganger. They were invariably employed directly by the company that got the contract, on proper insurance, cards, pay-as-you-earn, everything regular and legit. Even if it was a new contract, they would go onto the job, hand their cards in, on the first day of the contract.

Graduate profession   By this time I was getting a bit fed up with the piecework. You'd maybe work hard and earn money a couple of days, then you'd get two or three days' rain and you couldn't work. And I thought, This is no good, I don't want to be working like this when I'm forty, never mind later on in life. The Sussex contract was coming up to change, and A.E. Bartholomew's came in and took over the contract from McCullough's. So I asked them if I could go on for them as a direct, proper, regular employee, as a pipelayer.

It seemed a big decision at the time. But once I'd made the change from being a self-employed pieceworker to working for the firm, it was almost like putting on a warm coat. You knew that it wouldn't totally safeguard you from insecurity, from getting the sack or whatever, but you were in a much better position than when you were self-employed. I worked with Bart's for eight years, from 1966 till 1974, the longest I ever worked for one civil engineering contractor. I was successively pipelayer, jointer and ganger.

This was the natural progression once you were employed by the firm. You would graduate. And nearly everybody, by the time they were forty, would either have got out of the game or would be gangers, or at least jointers. And would not be expected to perform like a navvy. Oh they would still get hold of a shovel and do a bit of this and that, but not the high-pressure work. It was like two separate parts of the gang, the so-called unskilled, and the skilled direct employees for the contractors.

Renaissance   Bart's was a good firm by anybody's standards but as well as that there was a sort of general renaissance in the gas industry at this time. British Gas tightened up on safety and insisted that contractors take on a certain percentage of direct-employed men. There was a move from self-employed to direct-employed conditions.

Pipelayer   The pipelayer was the bottom of the legit hierarchy on the gang. His job was to prepare the bed of the trench for the pipe. They were eighteen or twelve foot cast-iron pipes in those days and had to lay on a flat, level bed, because cast is quite brittle and if there was a depression or a hump, they could break their backs.

The pipelayer also had to make sure the bed of the trench had the correct slope on it, because in those days with iron pipes they had to go to a specific fall. In the old days before natural gas, it was coal gas, which was a damp gas, so there would be a residue of moisture in the pipe. And because you had to lay to a fall, this moisture would end up in traps, what we call siphons, at various places, always at the lowest point. And where the siphon was there would be a small box where they could pump the water out from time to time into a tanker. The box would only be about six inches square. You still see them all over the place now, they haven't taken a lot of them out.

The pipelayer would also assist the jointer. His responsibility was to actually do up the joints of the pipe and make sure that he had leakproof joints, that was vital. The pipelayer assisted him in getting the pipe from where the pipes were stacked, manhandling it into the trench, cleaning it, both the spigot and the socket, putting all the nuts and bolts out ready for the jointer, and his tools. Then he would help the jointer push the pipe home into the socket of the previously laid pipe. If the pipes were very heavy, eight-inch cast-iron and up, then probably the pieceworker would be involved with this as well. He also had to dig a little bit out the side of each trench so that when the pipes were put together the jointer could get his spanner in. Sometimes you couldn't help laying the pipe with a bolt underneath it, so then the pieceworker had to dig a joint-hole. The ganger would help the jointer as well, there wasn't any sort of demarcation lines, really. Especially if you got on with everybody in the gang.

Taxman   So, I started working as a pipelayer. And it was OK. My money was not any less than I was getting as a pieceworker and it was guaranteed, plus holiday money, paid days off for public holidays and that sort of thing. I think even in the first year I was in front as far as money was concerned. Plus having the security and my National Insurance and all that paid up.

There was a bit of a problem with the tax first of all, because when I worked for the subbie we hadn't been paying any tax. I wouldn't have paid a lot anyway, with what I was getting. But I got over that by going into the tax office and acting like a sort of dopey incoherent Irishman. Which worked. They sort of acted as if I was more trouble than I was worth. They dismissed me, they said, All right, we'll start from scratch. It doesn't always pay to be a smart-arse. I'd kept up my National Insurance, paid the self-employed stamp, I think it was eighteen shillings a week. I knew that was absolutely sacrosanct, you had to do that.

Falling out over a windywheel Then I fell out with the ganger. I can remember distinctly what it was over. Whereas before I'd worked with this same guy as a pieceworker, as a pipelayer I wasn't quite as quiet and prepared to accept things. And this particular occasion, the jointer was cutting a pipe with what we call a windywheel, which is a very high speed pneumatically driven cutting disc, like an angle-grinder. It's hand-held and it's a dangerous tool. Quite recently a guy on one of the other gangs, one of these wheels had shattered, had chopped right through to his jaw and opened his face up really badly. It was only the fact that he had quite a dewlap, that he didn't sever his jugular vein. And our jointer who was using one of these windywheels didn't have any goggles on. So I said to the gangerman, Why hasn't he got any goggles? And he said, Listen, I decide what's what, he said, and I'm the ganger. So then I just piped up, said, Well you should start acting like a ganger then, Mick. And one thing led to another and I was put with another gang as a pipelayer.

Uncle George The ganger was George Deakin, we called him Uncle George. Very nice guy, English guy, ex-matelot, he's dead now. And I got along with George very well. I liked him, he was the best ganger I worked with actually. Very funny man, full of Navy stories. He didn't push, and he worked very hard. And we did have a lot of fun with him.

Then his pipe-jointer left and I became a jointer, and after I'd been a jointer for a couple of months, my mate Dan was looking for a job, so I got him on with us as a pipelayer. So it was like the old team again.

And again we used to get up to a lot of nonsense. I remember we used to try and wrap the job up on Friday lunchtime, and we'd have a drink at the pub. Then go back to the job and just clear up, put the fences up and that sort of thing. And one particular occasion we were working on a long pipeline from Castletown to Small Dole, and we'd been to the Rising Sun on the Steyning road and had a few beers, and that afternoon Dan and I were trying to rope these bullocks in a field and ride 'em, we got torn to bits. We managed to get the ropes round their necks and then he got dragged through gorse and bristles and Christ knows what. And that was quite funny. But it's just one thing and the other.

And that was a good time for us. Money wasn't bad. It wasn't fantastic, but it was regular. I worked with George for about a year.

GANGERMAN

Up the ladder   The Bartholomew's agent came to me and said,
Did I think I could take a gang? I hadn't been critical of George
but I'd been critical of about nearly every other ganger I'd worked
with, so I thought, Well I can't really open my mouth and be critical about people if I'm not prepared to have a go myself and take
the responsibility that other people have had. So I became a ganger.
Which meant a rise in money, and obviously a rise in status. I'd
never had such an exalted position. I would have been in my late
twenties.

My first job as ganger was working in Worthing, the road where
Worthing Hospital is, on what they called leak clamps. You dig
down on an existing pipe, usually quite big pipes, eighteen inches
diameter. These are the old lead joints, and they were all leaking.
You go down, dig round the joint, you then get what they call a
set which is a plumber's tool, you go all the way round the lead,
banging it back with a hammer – or dressing it, I think that might
be the term. Then you put a rubber gasket round that and a clamp
to hold it all in. Theoretically it'll stop the leaking. And that was
my first job as a ganger.

When I first became a ganger at Worthing, I had two mates of
mine with me, because Dan became my jointer, and this other
guy Lou, an old mate of mine, he became the pipelayer.

Now Lou's the guy that went hod-carrying, got the hod stuck
in his wellington and shot the pug all over the bricklayer. So Lou
is clumsy. Anyway the first day he started with me – this is hard
to believe – he fell out of a hole, he knocked a bucket of soapy
water over one of the labourers down one of the other holes, he
nearly brained himself walking into our aluminium shed and not
ducking, and then tipped all of the fried bread and stuff out of
the frying pan, looking at his watch. And this was all before half-
past ten on a Monday morning. I thought, My God, what have
I got here? The catastrophes did taper down a bit but Lou was
always very very clumsy and awkward. But again it was quite fun
working with him.

Gangerman and the men When I became a ganger I had to learn to handle men myself. You have to adopt certain attitudes, you can't be a bully, and then you can't be too soft, you've got to build yourself up a bit of a reputation. And I think that I've got quite a good reputation amongst the guys that have worked under me, all the years.

It's a matter of having their respect, and to a degree, an amount of affection. I would do certain things, sometimes they would respond and sometimes they wouldn't, but they'd always give me the benefit of the doubt. For example, it would be one of those depressing January mornings and I might have four or five guys working in the trench. It would be raining, not enough to drive us off into the shed or back home, but it would be quite miserable. And I'd walk up and down the trench where the lads were all digging and say, Right, no singing. That's not strictly my own invention, it was inspired by a Giles cartoon in the *Express*, one of these dour, miserable English pubs, with a real miserable-looking landlord and a couple of fogies in the corner, and there'd be a notice up in the bar saying, No singing. And no one ever tumbled that I was being very very sarcastic, but nevertheless they never got mad. Possibly they did tumble, maybe I'm not giving them enough credit.

Deaf Tony Tony the deaf jointer was a very nice guy, very good at his job. He was strong and physical and liked to make things. He was very good at woodwork and shuttering and that sort of thing. But I'd had no experience of deaf people prior to this. I don't know sign-language and when I spoke to him I would be mouthing slowly, with exaggerated lip movements. He could lipread, at that pace. But the noises he made back were far louder than the noises I was making. He could form a few simple words, in a hoarse, strained voice, semi-articulated. Like, NO GOOD, FUCK OFF. There's no subtleties, things are black, or they're white.

Sometimes it used to be almost heartbreaking. If I was very busy I'd see him throwing things about. And I'd go up to him and I'd say, What's the matter? And he said, You don't talk to me any more, you're ignoring me. And unless it happened to be something very specific like measurements, he wouldn't have things written down, no matter what. He was very stubborn. I mean if we'd have an argument, the way that he would finish it, he'd turn away. So I had to consciously make sure he was aware that I was not forgetting him, all the time.

Once it got to be quite a heated argument between us and in the end I wrote in big letters in chalk on the road, You're answerable to me, I'm not answerable to you, if you don't like it, eff off. And that's what I wrote, in twelve-inch letters in the road in Southwick. And he looked at it, and I saw his brain was ticking over, and then he picked up the shovel and carried on working.

Talking it through   But I think I've only ever sacked two people. One was a guy from Donegal who came to work so drunk he kept falling over and then turned awkward when I told him to go home and sleep it off. The other was an English-Irish lad. When the job got particularly bad he decided he wasn't coming in, he'd got a cold, but he was back in again when we'd done the worst of it. And I just went up to the agent, I said, Right, I'm not having him with me. So there's only two. Which is not bad in thirty years.

How many people have I had working under me? Oh God, I should think a couple of hundred, maybe. Quite a lot. I could usually talk to guys, and I've had quite a lot of pretty aggressive guys, pretty uptight guys sometimes, especially when their money's been wrong. And often their money has been wrong, they've been fiddled, one way and the other. Or they've misunderstood something. I found that the so-called thickies, they're not thick, at all, if you take the trouble to try and talk in their language, or see things from their point of view. Then you can usually come to some sort of agreement with them.

I've had very few confrontations. I've had lots with management, an awful lot. And with members of the public. But not with the actual guys that worked with me. One or two with dogs, but that's off the record.

Irishmen   There used to be an awful lot of Irish characters round Brighton. And a lot of very hard men. On one of my jobs as a labourer, I worked for Murphy's laying cable, there must have been fifty or sixty men there. They were building a big electricity generating station at Bolney. And there was myself and a Scotsman, all the rest were West of Ireland Gaelic-speaking. And it is a bit unnerving to be with that many people that are speaking a language you don't understand.

They were rough, they are definitely rough. But I didn't get any nonsense. Once when they came back from the pub I was in the back of this lorry with one other guy. As they drove out of the field – I thought they were only pretending to be pissed – they turned the lorry over. Not very comfortable, no. There was trees there, it went over on its side, it couldn't roll completely over, that was the only reason we were saved. And the guy that was with me in the back, who was nicknamed The Pig, he got out of the lorry, felt himself, and then the last I saw of him he was running down the road and shouting, Jesus, they're trying to kill us. And I never saw him again, I don't think he even went back for his wages.

These Gaelic speakers, their English was OK, with an accent. And quite frankly, for the most part they were better spoken than an awful lot of working-class Englishmen, the vocabulary seemed better.

Englishmen tend to have this stereotypical picture of a buffoon of an Irishman, but they're not like that at all. One of the first things English people do, they stick a name on anyone that's not from England, like they used to call them Taffy, or Pat, or Jock. Now some of these people's names *are* Pat, Taffy or Jock. But you should find out what they are called. Whenever a guy came on a job I found out what his name is, and when they were subcontract I always said, I don't want to know your surname, because if I don't know it I don't have to lie about it if anybody asks me, taxman, whatever.

Older generation   A number of the Irishmen that I worked with would have been of the generation born around the early twenties, maybe fifteen years older then me, that came over on their own and lived in lodgings or rooms.

They weren't married, they lived in a rotten flat, the pub was their social life. But they weren't alcoholics as some people think every Irishman is. They worked very hard in harsh conditions that most Englishmen wouldn't tolerate. Which is why I think a lot of them have died.

They would sometimes be working together as a group and they brought their culture with them, as well as their own language. The agents had to be very careful how they spoke to them. Most of the time, the ganger would be one of their own, like if they were Connemara men, he would be a Connemara man. You would very seldom get an Englishman telling a whole gang of Irishmen what to do. It just didn't happen.

Sometimes they would be fiddled because they weren't good at figures or whatever, but if they did know their money was wrong then the reaction was invariably physical, and quick.

There's not the wild men about that there used to be, which I regret quite frankly because I like those wild men. Once you cease to be intimidated by them – and they were intimidating believe you me – and knew them, they were fine, fine men. Especially those from the west of Ireland and the islands.

The ones that have come over since, the next generation down, don't come from such hard backgrounds because obviously things in rural Ireland have improved no end, so they're not the real rock-hard, tough boys from the farms and the bogs. They tend more to be tradesmen as opposed to just buck navvies. They're guys my age or younger, most of them have got a mortgage, they've got kids.

Long John   One of the older generation was a guy called Long John, an Irish guy and a well-known character on all the gangs. He wouldn't do much, but some people said it was worth having him on a gang just for the crack, because he was so funny. One day we were working in Brighton and he was doing the lamps. Now in the old days when they were paraffin lamps, it was a filthy job and you can't help but get your hands dirty. So the way we used to do it was to get a bucket of paraffin and just dip the container in to fill it up. It was the quickest way, instead of using a jug or a funnel. Anyway one day a woman saw him doing this and she said, My goodness, my man, you're not going to make the tea in that bucket are you? He said, Jesus no, madam, he says, There's a lot of us on the job today, we're going to make it in a wheelbarrow. He wouldn't work hard, but I mean who can blame him for that, for God's sake?

I think he died of pneumonia. But again probably through a sort of self-neglect.

Pappy   Old Pappy Fogerty was another of them. I knew him, oh for thirty years, but he didn't work with me until quite late in his working life. He came from a family in Clare which is a very hostile county.

121

Pappy was one of two brothers, his brother had married and got a couple of kids, and when the father died, the farm wasn't big enough to support two brothers. And this often happened, because Ireland was broken up into lots of small bits of land. So Pappy came to England. That was very sad. He got on with the English and everybody liked him. His nickname among the Irish guys was The Vicar, anybody in Brighton would know him as The Vicar, because you'd never hear him swear. He wasn't a Holy Joe or anything like that but he was a very even-tempered man, and I never saw him get excited or really badly lose his temper, no matter how adverse things were going.

His social life was totally the pub. He didn't drink a lot, but that's what he did, and he lived in a poxy little one-room flat up near Hove Station, which was pretty wretched. I visited him there once or twice, and it was just this bare room, it wasn't dirty or anything, it was just drab and mean, the decor was awful. But that's where he used to spend his time. And then he developed kidney trouble, so he couldn't drink at all. And I used to think, My God, the poor bugger, living in this rotten room, sitting up there night after night. No television, nothing but the radio.

Pub was the home. I don't know if there is an alcohol problem with Irishmen, but that's where they used to meet, that was their club, that was their focal point. So Pappy used to go down the pub. He would go for walks around the town. When he was all dressed up you'd think he was a bank clerk or something. He was always smart and well turned-out. He used to smoke an awful lot. It was impossible to do it at work but weekends he used to smoke about eighty Senior Service a day.

He had a very good name, he was a very conscientious guy, one of the best jointers I've ever worked with. But he would also work as a labourer, and never complained. The ganger that he worked with for many years was George Deakin, the one we called Uncle George.

Bad dreams   It was much later, when I was the ganger on this quite extensive pipeline that went right across the Royal Eastbourne golf course, that Pappy was first sent to work with me as a jointer. Later still, when my gang were working on a large diameter job in Horsham, he nearly lost a finger. It's a long story but basically it was my fault. I was trying to hurry the job on. Although I didn't see it happen, in hindsight I sort of knew that when that pipe thudded, that was his finger coming off, and I often had bad dreams about that. After it happened I was in shock, I kept saying, You're going to be all right Pappy, you're going to be all right Pappy. And he said, Yeah, and how would I be all right with my fucking finger off? I remember that as clearly as anything, that he had the asperity to answer like that. Anyway the guy took him to hospital in Crawley, and I couldn't leave the job because we were in the middle of it.

They put the finger back and he was OK, he didn't hold it against me. I said, Well Paps, I think this is the time now when you really should try and get out of this game. And he said, Well no, I can't give up the work, Peter, because it's my life now. Because of this ongoing kidney problem I've got, I can't go to the pub, not that I used to drink much anyway, but that was my social life, and going to work is the only means I have of contact with other people. He said, I've got to do the job, it keeps me sane.

Home to County Clare

But in the end he hasn't come back to work, the firm have finished him up, he's been paid a couple of thousand quid compensation, which I was very pleased that he'd got. He's accepted his retirement and gone back to Ireland. The money was enough for him to buy a small cottage in Clare, near his brother's farm, so he was back among his own folk.

Wendy and I went to see him in Ireland. He hadn't been well and when he came to the door he said, You never expected to see me walking with a stick Peter. But he was content. He made us tea, made us

12. *Peter visiting Pappy in his cottage at Ballyconnoe, County Clare, 9 August 1990.*

very welcome, and showed us with great pride his store of winter fuel which was turf, or peat as we call it. And he insisted we have a very strong shot of Irish whisky, and chat. We didn't stay too long, an hour or so, and I was giving him all the gossip about what was going on here, in the job.

And a couple of years afterwards I got a Mortuary Card, one of those little things the Catholics send, it's the notification of a mass said for somebody. And he'd died, on 23 January 1993. Which was very sad. But I was just glad that he did get two years back home, where he wanted to be, with who he wanted to be, because I did dread the thought of him dying in that poxy little flat by Hove Station.

He's one of the nicest, most gentle men that I've ever met, and particularly in our job, gentle men are not everyday things, you just don't meet them. He would have made a wonderful father or grandfather. Which he didn't, he never married. A wonderful man. Who'd never achieved anything in life, apart from being an excellent worker, really well thought of, and liked and loved by a lot of people. And really, what else can one ask for?

Deadmen tell no tales   When I was first made up to be a ganger I was given a block of sheets, like a big writing pad, massive thing. Four copies of each sheet, so there were three carbon sheets. They were pre-formatted and I just had to fill them in – the personnel on the job, what their trades were, the plant on the job, and what work was done, on a daily basis. And sign down at the bottom right-hand corner.

And the first Friday the company agent came round and said, All right, I'll take your worksheets, Peter. I said, Oh I'll fill 'em up, I can take them home at the weekend. He said, No you don't want to be bothered with that, I'll take 'em. So I let it go, I thought, Well that's nice of him. Anyway the following Monday, he'd torn off the sheets, I just looked at the imprint of the writing, just casually. And I thought, Hang on. In the personnel section I could see the imprint of two more names. I thought, What is going on here?

Then I remembered years ago when I was a pieceworker the gangerman sending me up to the local gas office with the worksheets, same type of sheets, and I'd looked at these sheets when I got round out of sight of the ganger, being curious, and saw there were two extra names on there, over and above the number of men that were in the gang. We were being kept very busy by that ganger, I mean there was no let-up. And it was obvious that we were kept busy to make up the work that these two fictitious guys would have done. But I couldn't do anything about it because the minute I opened my mouth I'd have just been told, Right, eff off, that would have been it. No redress, no appeal, nothing.

So anyway, coming back to that first weekend I was a ganger, I thought, The bastard, he's taking the piss. So on the following Friday when the agent came in again, I was sitting in the shed, writing something in my daily log, and he said, Oh, I've come for the sheets Peter. I said, That's all right John, I said, I'll do them. He said, No no I'll do them, you don't want to be bothered with that, go on, I'll do them over the weekend. I said, No John, I've got the work written out in rough here in my own log-book, I'll do the sheets.

So he in the meantime tried to pick them up, and I've got hold of one corner and he'd got hold of the other. And I wouldn't let go, and he was sort of gently tugging. He said, Oh don't mess about, give them here. I said, No John, I said, I think you're taking the piss. And he looked at me what seemed like ages, stared straight into my eyes. And I didn't flinch. And he knew that I knew. He then said, Oh there's a little matter I want to discuss with you Peter. And that's when I got into the deadman's scheme. The only difference being that I used to split up the extra money with all the other guys on the gang. Which wasn't bad. If you oil the wheels they go round a bit smoother.

There again, I didn't really have any choice. If I'd have got sniffy and said, I won't be part and parcel of this, you will NOT add the fictitious names to the sheets, then my career as a ganger would have been very short-lived. I would have been got rid of under some pretext very quickly. But anyway the company later put a stop to all that.

Healthy competition   Another job as gangerman for Bart's was at Sussex University, laying a new main on the perimeter road up there. And a guy called Eddy Clancy and another guy, Johnny Leary, were sent out to me as labourers.

I'd already encountered Clancy some years before when he was the ganger and I was the only pieceworker and he sat in his car and watched me digging, on this vast estate out at Eastbourne. So when Clancy and this other guy were sent out to me as labourers I thought, Right. My mate Dan was working with me then as my jointer. I didn't have a pipelayer. So they were going along the top, taking the top eighteen inches out, digging, and then Dan and I were coming along taking the next bit. But I was really forcing the pace, we were up behind them so they couldn't stop for breathers or anything, I was really forcing the pace.

And on the Thursday, I'd gone to phone up the firm saying I wanted pipes or something or other, and Clancy started moaning to Dan. Now Clancy didn't realise how thick Dan and I were, because when we're together we quite often don't give that impression. We'll argue, quite heatedly, but I mean we've knocked about for forty years. So anyway he said, Well Christ Almighty, how much more does he want done this week? So Dan said, Oh, he got through eighteen bloody labourers in that St James Street job – that was another job I'd been running that was quite busy. So Clancy says, Well he won't get through me like that, I'll put him in the trench first. So Dan says, Yeah, that's the way to talk to him, that's the sort of language he understands. I didn't know anything about this till afterwards.

Anyway we finished that day, and on the Friday morning Clancy and his mate didn't show up till about nine o'clock. He then rolled up with his mate and I could see them getting their boots and working gear out of the shed. So anyway when he drove up alongside the trench where we were working I said, Are you jacking then, Clancy? So he said yes. I said, Well it's a pity you didn't tell me that yesterday, I could have got another couple of skins up here today to replace you. Skins being a word we use for men. At this point Clancy jumped out of his car and said, Well I'm not staying here and being ordered around by a cross-eyed English bastard like you.

I thought, he's a bit of a fool, I hadn't ordered anybody about, I always ask people to do things anyway. Anyway he made a jump towards me. I thought, My God he really wants to mix it, so I didn't hesitate, I just threw off my glasses with my left hand and threw a right, and caught him just above his right eye. He went back up against his car and I saw a little trickle of blood come out between his fingers, and he said, Right, that's all I wanted. So Dan, who was standing there, said, If that's all you wanted, Clancy, you could have had it last Monday. Then Clancy said, Oh that's it, I'm going to call the police now. I said, Hey, you're too thick to remember the number Clancy.

So he got in his car and drove off. I said, Now, that's great, what brought all that on then? Dan said, Oh, I was winding Clancy up yesterday. And he repeated what he'd said to Clancy. I said, Christ Almighty, suppose it had gone the other way? He said, It couldn't have done, I was ready with the shovel. And that was the end of that little episode. Then we had to clear up for the rest of the day there, and I got another couple of guys out with me Monday.

New contracts When a contract is coming to an end the incoming contractor has always visited the site and asked if I would be prepared to work for them. Then would follow a discussion about wages etcetera. They usually paid exactly the same as I was receiving from my previous employer, although in the some cases the incoming contractor paid a lot less.

The reason the new contractor knew where to find certain gangs was that he would have had a meeting with the SEGAS District Engineer who would unofficially recommend certain mainlayers that he knew and approved of and would be pleased if the new contractor would employ these men. It would be a brave or foolish man that dare defy this engineer, whose word was law. This could work the other way: if a particular mainlayer had upset the same district engineer, though not enough to be sacked for bad work, it could be a purely personal thing, then a quiet word to the new contractor and the man would not be taken on. You can take an employer to a tribunal for unfair dismissal but not for failing to employ you. This was and is a covert way of blacklisting a man.

Working for British Gas I would be dealing for the most part with the same British Gas engineers. And I've often stated, much to the annoyance of whichever company I worked for, Really, you're only the person that brings me my wages on a Friday, you're virtually irrelevant. As far as I'm concerned, I work for British Gas, I'm working on their stuff and to the standard that they want.

This system, of which I can't approve, stood me in good stead for many years, as I always kept my nose clean as far as the District Engineer was concerned. Although I was on the carpet for various acts of insubordination, it was never through bad or incompetent workmanship.

With all these different companies I've worked for, we would be in the middle of a job, and we'd go home Friday working for one firm, and come back on the Monday working for another. We'd have to go to a different yard and pick up a new van, and the tools, but it was the same job. Different company, same hole.

On a Monday, there was very seldom any actual supervision directly on the job from anybody higher up from me. The supervisors would come once a day for the most part, but sometimes I wouldn't see a supervisor for a week, and nowadays, you can go two weeks and not see one at all. Which has got very bad. On important jobs, important big connections, there would be engineers, there'd sometimes be three or four people on site that were what I would call non-productive, from British Gas and the company that I would be working for. In fact this used to be embarrassing. There's been as many as four pristine dayglo jackets hanging over the fence watching two of us down a hole, working.

Family firm   In 1974 the contract changed and was taken over by a firm called E. W. Avent. I continued to work for them as a ganger, until 1977.

Avent's was a family firm, one of the old firms. And unlike nearly all the other firms, they took health and safety quite seriously. The father had started the company, and his son was a director. And they were very nice people, I must admit. It was during their employ that I was to have a cataract operation, and they were concerned, and they came round and saw me while I was off. And you could speak to the actual boss of the firm, a guy called Eddy Avent, who everybody regarded as a gentleman. I don't know what a gentleman is, but he was always pleasant to me and one didn't have to touch one's forelock, metaphorically or literally, when he came round the job. I think it was the last of the family-type firms in the business. I think they were bought out by another big company and split up, though not in the Sussex contract I worked on. Which I was sad to see, because I quite liked Avent, and could talk to the man.

University yahoos   We did quite a lot more work up the University. And from working on that perimeter road we went on to lay some gas mains up round those sort of houses where families of students or whatever live, right up the north end of the University, I think they call it the Village.

But quite frankly some of the students were a bloody nuisance, we had more vandalism and trouble on that campus than we had at Whitehawk, Moulsecoomb or any of the so-called rougher estates. And we had to keep a sort of security patrol up for several weeks, till the end of term.

Another thing that used to really get up our nose, we were hand-digging on that job and it was hot, and we were going up round the back of the Residences, and in the afternoons especially when it was getting really hot, round about half-past two, three o'clock time, we were digging away and they would come out – ah good luck to them really – with their stereos and their speakers out on long leads, and cold drinks, and be chatting there and having the crack, and I didn't see anybody seriously studying, maybe because it was near the end of term, but we did feel a bit envious of that I must admit.

A grave business   When we finally finished at the University, the Marina was starting. And we were doing a lot of work diverting gas mains along the cliff-tops there, into Rifle Butt Road, that's up beside the big block of flats called Marine Gate. We did an awful lot there, in the gasworks at Black Rock and out in that road. It was being demolished to make way for the approach roads to the Marina. I think that was not long before natural gas came in.

There was a Quaker graveyard there and when they exhumed the graves, there was one more grave there than they'd got records for. And where our trench had come through, a very deep trench, where the cut had been done you could see quite distinctly the sort of vertical rectangle of where the graves had been, down six foot. They were all pretty uniform, but a couple were deeper, I don't know if that's where they'd done a family thing and buried one on top of the other.

And we kept finding what I thought were old-fashioned galvanised-iron baths. They looked like the old baths you used to hang up outside the back door and people used to bath in, in front of the fire. And my mate Dan, who is always curious, got one of these and opened it up. I think it was zinc. And it was coffin-

13. The highly skilled work of wrapping a 'hot tap' which has been precision-welded onto a live gas main: Peter oversees on the right, July 1979.

liners. He even found some rib-bones in one of them, for Christ's sake, they were rib-bones of either a child or a woman. But anyway that's another story.

Death on Marina site   But prior to us doing that job a guy down the Marina had been killed. They hit the medium-pressure gas main there. They were breaking up concrete down below the cliff with what we call a pecker, which is a big thing on the end of a digger arm, like a great big pneumatic drill. They'd been told exactly where this gas main was, but this guy had gone through this main with it. There was a perfect hole about two-and-a-half inches in diameter. And the gas came screaming out of there, and the noise would have been horrifying, and it caught light, so you'd got like a bloody great gas jet roaring away, really roaring. And he backed his machine out of the way and a JCB driver, thought he was going to put the fire out, got a big scoop of dirt and chalk with his front bucket, came along to douse the flame with it. Which is totally the wrong thing to do anyway. But instead of coming along and pushing it from the ground level onto the leak, he went to tip the earth down from above. What that did, that diverted the flame jet straight back at the cab, and virtually cooked him inside the JCB. He was still alive I think on the way to the hospital but he was breathing out gas and flame, it was that bad. If he'd pushed it, well, he might have been OK.

But the thing to do when a gas main's alight like that, you leave it burning. You know where it is, the gas is being burned up, it can't cause an explosion, it's safe. It's not nice, it's frightening, with the noise and everything, but it's safe. Then you go further back up the line from where the puncture is, it takes quite a few hours, dig down, shut the gas off, and you're OK. But he thought he was doing the right thing.

I wasn't there on that particular incident, but we were doing work on that same main and I saw the piece of pipe that came out from there, I knew all about it afterwards. But it was all, as usual, kept pretty quiet. But in essence that's what happened.

Eviction   Another disquieting incident that happened on that same job, Dan and I were coming to work one morning, into the north gate of the gasworks, and we looked down this unmade road, at the back of Arundel Road, and saw all this furniture out.

I thought, What the hell's that, and this I think was in February. It was pretty cold anyway. And Dan says, Huh, that looks like a bloody eviction to me. So we just strolled down there, as usual, we're nosy, and curious – he was nosy, I was curious – and saw all this furniture stacked out. And first of all we didn't notice this woman. But in a chair there was this old woman, with God knows how many blankets round her. And we said, What's up, love, what's going down? So she said, Oh, you don't want to hear my troubles. Oh come on, what's the problem, what's up, have you been thrown out like this? She said, Well my landlord's evicted me, the day before yesterday, and put all my stuff out here, and I was staying somewhere else, but I came back to look at my stuff, and some of it's been pinched. I said, Been pinched? She says, Yes, she said, I've got it back, some of my ex-neighbours have had stuff. She'd been out all night watching it.

Brown-ricers   So I said, Ah Jesus Christ, we can't have this, we've got to do something. So I knew some people who in those days were sometimes written off as freaks, sort of semi dropouts, student-type, druggy-type people that used to congregate at a place called Open in Victoria Street, Brighton, which was like a café or restaurant, they used to have health food and home-made stuff. We called 'em brown-ricers. There was a guy there called Bruno. So I rang Bruno and I said, Look I don't know if you can do anything about this but you know how to help people, you have all these sort of help lines and things. I've got a lady here, she's been evicted, she's got all her stuff out, neighbours have been pinching her stuff, last night she spent sitting in a chair out of doors. This is in bloody February, I said, This can't go on.

So he said, Right. I told him where it was and he got it all organised that day, got her somewhere else to stay, got a couple of vans, got all her furniture and stuff and put it in store, and that was the last I heard of it. I expect that sort of nonsense from landlords, but for neighbours to start pilfering from someone you've said Good morning to for maybe a couple of years, that's really dirty. OK, when she'd started making a fuss they gave it back, and there were excuses, Oh we're looking after it, whatever, but that was disgusting.

Anyway she was taken care of by the so-called freaks and drop-outs. Open was a kind of community café. Wendy used to go there and take the kids sometimes. They organised all sorts of things. That were quite good, and some of the people who used to go there we are still friends with.

Pipe dance   Another thing that happened at Black Rock, we were sort of attached to another part of the firm. There was quite a few guys working there and I was in charge, because I'd had the experience of working on quite large schemes and large-diameter pipework. And there was one occasion, Dan was with me, we were down in this trench. And the digger was lowering in this eighteen-foot, twelve-inch diameter iron pipe. And all of a sudden the pipe started to jump up and down. I yelled at the digger driver asking him what the so-and-so he thought he was doing. And what had happened, he'd shouted some insult to one of the guys on the job. They said he was a Canadian Indian, he was called Joe. And this guy had run up the arm of the digger bucket, that was lowering the pipe to us, and was trying to kick this digger driver, who's sat there with all the levers in front of him. And he's trying to kick this guy but he's kicking the levers. And we were in the trench with this half a ton of pipe bouncing up and down, actually in between us, Dan was one side of the trench, I was on the other.

So I've leapt out the trench and I've calmed this bloke down. I said, Joe, if you're going to kill him, let him lower the pipe in, then drag him out the machine, take him down the road and kill him, but for Christ's sake, you haven't got anything against us two. And after that I had to keep that guy very very separate from the digger driver. But anyway, he calmed down. And he went away.

Natural gas   The conversion to natural gas had started to come through Brighton in the early seventies, when they started putting the natural gas section valves through. As I say this was part of a wider renaissance in the gas industry which I experienced when I was working with Bart's. The whole gas scene changed. Conditions and standards of work improved, there was an end to cowboy employers and we got more sophisticated equipment, like we no longer had to use a thing like a football bladder inside a canvas bag to stop the gas off.

The only thing that didn't change at that time was the basic structure of the gangs, they still had a couple of self-employed or subcontract labour.

Technically things had to be changed for the better because with natural gas all the pipes, both the big ones and the small ones running up the streets, were working at much higher pressure. As I say, the old-fashioned coal gas was wet, there was a lot of moisture in it. Now, the joints on the old mains were lead, and when you made a lead joint you used hemp, before the lead was run, so the hemp in the joints would stay swollen. But natural gas is dry, you do not have moisture collecting. So it was drying out the hemp in all these old joints, in pipes from three inches to forty inches, and there was an awful lot of leaks. An awful lot of leaks. With the extra pressure and the fact that it was dry gas.

And then I started working on what they called section valves. The natural gas came along section by section, a section valve for every three thousand consumers. As the natural gas came through, it pushed the old gas up against the new section valve, which was closed. The old gas was then burned off before we went on to the next stage. That's how it worked. And this was quite a nerve-racking job inasmuch that I hadn't had any experience of this particular branch of work before. The first big job we did was in Southwick which was a double valve insertion.

Cracking the whip   Because the pressure on the overall mains had to be cut down, we used to do these section valves at night. Which involved lots of teams of guys controlling pressures round various parts of the town and the country. A lot, a lot of very careful organisation. Then we would cut these bits out on these large-diameter pipes. And on these night jobs we would double up on the gangs. I'd have another ganger and jointer and his men, with me, on my job. Anyway one night we were working on a job along Marine Parade, and we'd cut the piece out, that had all gone well, put the new components in, and then let the bit of gas through to test to see if the joints held. They wouldn't hold. And this was about two o'clock in the morning. We'd worked all that day and then into the night as well. We've got the natural gas flowing through but there's a leak.

So, about half-past two in the morning I climbed out the trench. I was very tired, and I said to Tom Chinchin who was my immediate supervisor from British Gas, I said, Tom, it won't hold, those components won't do, we'll have to do it in lead. We can make it safe for the night but I'm sorry, we've tried, and tightened up everything, and changed it, and done this, that and the other. So he turned round to the British Gas engineer that was in charge of the natural gas coming through. This was a man called Ian Kay, a rugby-playing Yorkshireman. Tom told him what the score was, although he'd obviously overheard what I was saying. He said, Right, get back in there and do what you can, he said, but crack the whip a bit will you? I couldn't believe it. We'd worked all day, half the night, and he's talking about cracking the whip.

So I went back down the trench and I turned to the others and I said, Did you hear all that, and they said, Yeah. I said, Will you back me up? They said, Yeah, whatever you like, we're not going to have that sort of nonsense. So I climbed back out the hole, talked to Tom Chinchin, who was standing within four foot of this Kay, who was looking really cheesed off, I said, Right Tom, either he gets back in his car and shuts up, or we walk off the job and leave it as it is now. We know we'll be sacked, we know we're going to be blacklisted, but we're not going to be spoken to like that. We're not a bunch of kids or cowboys. So Kay obviously had heard this, didn't say a word, got back in his car. So we then wrapped up the job and made it safe.

Cunning bastard   And we had to be back on the job the next morning, half-past seven, to do the same thing but with lead joints, which would take up all the inconsistencies and irregularities in the pipe. So we come back on the next morning, got all the lead gear out, ready to get the stoves going, all the rest of it. Kay said, Right, how long's this going to take? I said, Phew, take all day. Because I wasn't feeling at all happy, I'd had barely half an hour's sleep. He said, Oh God, well I tell you what, Richards, you get me back indoors for the rugby international at half-past three, he said, and I'll pay you and your men till six o'clock. So I said, Yeah, all right. And we wrapped the job up by half-past ten. He came up to me and said, You cunning bastard. My reply was, All sorts of things could have gone wrong. But he kept his word and paid us till six o'clock. And that's when my relationship with him changed for the better. He wrote me a couple of good references.

Fishing   New Steine was the first time I started to get involved with fishing boats. Boats were the second most important thing in my life after Wendy and the kids. When I first came to Brighton I used to fantasise about how wonderful it would be to go on one of the boats or go fishing.

Ten years later I did, and it was phenomenal, phenomenal. It was in the late sixties, when my wages got a bit better. I found out that you could buy boats off Brighton Council. They had been abandoned and left on the beach and were impounded for a year and then auctioned.

The first boat I had was an eight-foot clinker-built dinghy with a hole in it, which I duly patched up with fibreglass and bought a second-hand small Seagull outboard motor and put it on the beach at Black Rock. And this satisfied me for a little while, but a small boat is very difficult to launch off the beach in bad weather, or any sort of weather at all, it's too small to go through the rollers.

I learned how to handle boats by trial and error and I gradually worked my way up. I bought another boat, which was a bit bigger, and ended up with a traditional Brighton beach boat, the Saul, fourteen foot with a counter stern and a brand-new outboard.

This was just beside the groyne at Peter Pan's. There were quite a few people with that type of boat down there, and it was a very good atmosphere because everybody helped everybody else. But even if you used someone else's winch it always needed at least two of you to get a boat up the beach and if you came in at low tide that beach could sometimes be very steep, depending on what the wind and tide had been doing. It's almost like a precipice sometimes.

Good marks   Fishing off that beach, the marks, which were the various spots for fishing, were quite close together, within two miles of the shore. There was one mark, I think it was called Sussex Square, which meant that you got the little, stumpy steeple church halfway down West Street over one of the minarets on the Winter Garden at the Palace Pier. You then got a church at the back of Kemp Town, I think it was St Mark's, over the third or fourth house in Chichester Terrace. And on that we've caught plaice, dog-fish, mackerel, codling, whiting, dabs, on that one mark in the same place on the same day. The ground was rocks amongst sand. And you had to be spot on, if you overshot by twenty or thirty metres you wouldn't catch much at all.

Me Mujer   There was invariably just my mate Alan and I that went out from there, and we were only fishing with a rod. Then in 1968 we decided we'd like something a bit bigger because all the year round we'd been launching the boat from the beach and in the winter it used to get really bloody cold, very cold. We used to take a little brazier out with us, with coke in it, in a tray mounted in water, but the fumes nearly killed us. So then we bought a thirty-one footer ship's life-boat, galvanised steel. Just the hull, no boards, and a Scammel petrol engine, for two hundred quid. I was the one that put the money up. We thought we could turn it into a fishing cruiser.

We moored it up the river in Shoreham and we worked on this boat for months and months, buying stuff and materials as we could afford it. Decked it, put steering gear in it, put a wheelhouse on it and named it Me Mujer which is Spanish for My Woman. Which is corny but seemed all right at the time. We took it to sea a couple of times but it wasn't any good. It had got no keel and no bilge-keels, it would almost go sideways across the bloody

14. *Peter on his boat* Treble Chance *with a forty-pound tope he caught on a rod, about 1971.*

water. It didn't steer, and it didn't stop very quick. It was a real pig.

Treble Chance   Anyway, after about a year I sold it. Now I had enough money to buy this boat at Newhaven, which was my first proper fishing boat, the Treble Chance. It was sound, it had an air-cooled Lister diesel and to me it was everything I wanted in a boat.

We brought it round from Newhaven on a Saturday, and although there was a near-gale blowing I didn't have any lack of confidence or fear at all. In fact Wendy came down and watched, I told her roughly what time we would be going past Kemp Town. She did see us but she said that half the time the sea was so lumpy we were disappearing, she was a bit worried. But the boat performed perfectly well, and we got into Shoreham and tied up, and that was my first trip in it and I was really pleased with the boat.

I didn't have a partner, Mark and Stewart used to come out with me, and various other people would go out. I then bought these second-hand trammel nets, much holed, and shot those weekends, or during the holidays, and fished. I never got a lot but it was very satisfying to haul up and get some fish. And crabs, I got quite a lot of crabs, which were a real so-and-so in the net.

Partnership   Then I got myself made voluntarily redundant by Bart's and another guy suggested we go into partnership, one share for the boat, one for me and one for him. So he put his nets in with mine and taught me how to make the trammel nets up properly. I worked on the nets in my basement flat in New Steine. There used to be nets stretched from right out the kitchen, right through the hall into the living room right through to the front door. If somebody came along when I was in the middle of hanging the net they'd have to come in through the window. My wife was very patient about that. Once we'd made them I got a friend to give me a lift over with a car. I didn't have a car, never had a car.

The idea being that as I wasn't working I could clean the nets, he would help shoot the nets and get them in first thing in the morning very early. He would then go to work and keep his wage, we would then sell the fish and split it appropriately between me, the boat and him. We would just use my boat. His didn't get off the beach, I think he grew flowers in it in the end.

But it didn't work out because I would go over to Shoreham maybe four or five in the morning, this is in March, and I'd get in the boat which was moored up beyond the footbridge, bring it downstream to the Kingston Wharf, and I'd sometimes be laying there in the bottom of the boat freezing and he wouldn't show up at all or would be too late to do it before he went to work.

Solo   So the partnership didn't work out and I went back to Barts. I obviously wasn't going to make a go of it full-time fishing. So I'd usually get someone to come out with me when I was hauling, because that's obviously when people were interested, they're not interested in the mundane thing of just going out shooting nets, but hauling was all right, especially if the weather was good.

The only problem I did have was when I wanted to sell fish at Brighton fishmarket and was told I couldn't do that unless I belonged to the Brighton Fishermen's Association. I didn't know any of the fishing families then, and didn't particularly want to spend time in pubs currying favour with people. So I had to hawk the fish around or sell it to people in the pub.

Christie Sue   Then I sold the Treble Chance for six hundred and fifty quid, which was two hundred more than I'd paid for it and in 1973 bought a boat I'd always admired called the Christie Sue, which was bigger. It was twenty-five foot on the waterline, and it was immaculate. I found I could get this marine mortgage and made an offer of two thousand which the guy accepted. I think he was glad to get rid of it, because he'd only been out in it once or twice. So I've got the boat and it had a thirty-horse Petter engine which was immaculate, I mean it had hardly been used. And the boat was really nice to handle, comfortable in rough weather, it would take more rough weather than I would be prepared to go out in, a lot more. And it was just like stepping from an Austin Seven into a Rolls Royce. As far as I was concerned it was the prettiest boat in Shoreham, at the time.

Again, I would take people out, usually two or three friends, especially in the summer, there's always people that would go fishing or hauling nets. Just to go out, they liked it. They'd take a bit of the catch, but not expect anything. I didn't really bother about selling fish after that. I had the Christie Sue for five years and we had a lot of good times out in that.

Offshore   Something happens when you go offshore. It's always aggravation when you're getting off the mooring and there's lots of other people going out, and you've got to be careful, you can't relax for a minute. And when you go out, you take on a new lot of responsibilities. If you've got people with you you can't be stubborn and say, Oh we're going to stay out or, We're going to take chances.

But once you clear the harbour mouth, especially on nice spring days, and you're heading out towards the sea – invariably we're heading out south westerly – then everything else seems to drop away, there seems to be no problems, they seem to be left behind you once you've cleared the harbour.

Going off Brighton beach very early on a summer Saturday morning, there's an interesting phenomenon. We would anchor into one of those marks that I've mentioned, not that far offshore, and it would be quiet. And gradually the noise from the town would pick up. You'd hear isolated things like a fire engine or a police car. But what really struck you was that after about nine o'clock you would begin to hear a roar, just a roar, and that's what you were aware you were living with, all of your life that you live in the town. You don't notice it when you're there but when you get out at sea you do.

Seven Stars   This was on the Bank Holiday Monday in 1974, when Wendy had gone with the kids for a holiday to Shrewsbury, and I couldn't go because the job had reached a crucial stage. Dan came over from Shoreham and persuaded me to come out for 'a quiet drink'. We did a few pubs, just observing other people as much as anything, and ended up in a big pub in Ship Street, the Seven Stars. I'd had about nine shorts and a couple of pints, but I wasn't out of it at all.

Dan had asked this girl to dance and I was just sitting at the table and I looked up and saw they had stopped dancing and there was three blokes standing round them. They were obviously the doormen, which is a euphemism for bouncers, and I thought, What's going on here? I put my glasses in my jacket pocket, took my jacket off and had it in my left hand, and walked on. So the spokesman for this trio said, We want you out. I said, What for? He said, Because you look like trouble. So I said to Dan, What's going on here? He said, I don't know. So I said to the girl, Has he been funny with you? And she says, No, nothing, I don't know what's going on. I thought, Well this is completely unjustified, we've done nothing, we've said nothing, we've not staggered or fallen about.

So then I started to get ratty, I said, OK you want us out, you put us out. Meantime, the assistant manager's come up and he said, Would you leave please, if we give you your entrance money back? So I thought, Well that's all right, it's getting near closing time anyway. So we then moved to the desk, where the till was, with an escort of the three 'doormen' and Dan was given an amount of money back by the girl. He put the money in his pocket, then got his hands under the desk, threw the whole lot up in the air, beer glasses flying, turned, grabbed me two-handed by my collar and my midriff, literally threw me at the three bouncers and the Assistant Manager, and took off out through the door.

So I got to my feet pretty quickly and went out after him. But as I was getting out through the doors I dropped my jacket, which has got my glasses in, and it was quite an expensive, trendy, leather-lookalike jacket. So I thought, Oh I'm not letting that go, and fought my way, literally, back in, and I'm now fighting with the three bouncers. I've got my jacket, and two or three of these doormen were still hitting. Then I've got out into Ship Street, and somehow one of them tripped me. I went down on my knees and I got a severe kicking in the back.

Then I started to get really mad, just threw the jacket in the road and said, Right then, come on. And Dan was standing just across the road, I think there was a Chinese restaurant there, this is at the entrance to the Lanes. He said, Quick, the Old Bill. So I've picked up my jacket and we've taken off through the Lanes, with the three bouncers, and this policeman, in hot pursuit. And I think they were all comfortable with the running bit. Well then, when we got to Market Street we noticed there was a police patrol car drawn across the road. So we've stopped dead. And this copper that was chasing us, PC French, he stopped, and I said, Right, we've run, we've stopped, now what?

British justice   So it was a night in the nick and a week or two later we had to go to the Magistrate's Court in Brighton. We'd been urged by the police to plead guilty, but I thought, No, sod it. I've had my nose clean as far as the police are concerned, for many,

many years and I really didn't want any sort of a record whatsoever. In any case, I was not guilty, I fought in self-defence. The
main charge was throwing glasses. And that brings to mind a picture of picking up glasses and throwing them in people's faces,
which is not what happened at all. There were glasses on that
counter which Dan had overturned, but no one had actually picked
up a glass and thrown it.

I'd appeared as the middle-aged respectable father in duffle coat
and polo-necked sweater, looking as unlike a hooligan on a Friday
night as possible. But Dan was wearing a pair of mustard-yellow
cowboy boots, midnight-blue flares, a jacket that made him look
about eight foot square, and an Anthony Eden Homburg hat worn
squarely on his head. When I saw him I said, For Chrissake man,
you're going to get us six months, tone it down a bit.

The prosecutor started really trying to provoke him but Dan,
who was obviously Irish by name and by nature if not by accent,
didn't lose his Irish rag at all. He had both hands up in the air, a
bit like Al Jolson, saying, Oh no squire, it wasn't like that at all.
Then it was our turn to cross-examine the girl cashier that was at
the desk where the glasses were thrown. Allegedly.

So I said, Now, I'm accused of throwing glasses, which hand
did I throw them with? She said, You threw them with your left
hand. I said, Well how did I manage to throw glasses with my left
hand when I was carrying my jacket in my left hand? So she said,
Well I don't know. I said, Well yes, you are in this court making a
sworn statement, now come on, this is very important. Did I throw
with with my right hand or my left hand, what are you saying
here? You're a witness, you're under oath. And she said tearfully,
I don't know, I didn't want to come here, I don't know which
hand.

Collapse of case. But the other funny thing was, they didn't even
go outside to deliberate. They said, Right, case dismissed. For both
of us, that's it, we were out. If it had been anything more serious
obviously I would have got a solicitor, but I thought we could handle that, in spite of being a bit scared by what they could do to us.

DIFFERENT COMPANIES, SAME HOLE

Working blind   When I was working for Avent's, I had a cataract. At the time, Wendy's aunt had died and her house had been sold and there was a couple of thousand quid. Which meant that we at long last had the possibility of getting a mortgage on a house, Worcester Villas in Hove. But my sight was getting very very bad, and we were negotiating this mortgage, and I knew that I couldn't get the mortgage if I was off sick because I couldn't see.

For months I went on working, and my eyes were awful. I couldn't see. I should never have been at work. Quite often if I crossed the road I used to brace myself for the impact of the car coming. And if we worked on live gas, especially at night, and I had to wear a gas-mask, I literally couldn't see a bloody thing, I just couldn't. I'm bad enough without my glasses anyway, but at that time it was ridiculous.

But I had a really good team. I had my mate Dan, that I'd known for a really long time, and Vinny, and other guys. And they really did support me. They didn't do my share of the work, but things that I should have spotted, they spotted, things that I couldn't see, they could see, and things that I might miss, they would cover for me, or point out, discreetly, that I'd missed so-and-so. And it was good.

And Dan always reminds me of the strokes that I used to pull, like if it it was a road job, I'd say at the end of the day, Right clear up, sweep the road, and make sure the footpath especially is clean, and I would walk up and down. And if I felt gravel under my feet I'd make them do it again, that sort of thing. Dan says he often used to hang his jacket on a fork and bugger off and I'd be shouting and swearing at this all the afternoon. But the reality is that that never happened.

Operation   We got the mortgage, moved into Worcester Villas and then I went off sick. Six or eight months prior to that I should have stopped. This was 1976. Anyway I went to the Sussex Eye Hospital and had this operation. I'd been told that there was a risk, and I was very very scared, because I'd only got the sight in

143

one eye and if something went wrong there that was it, there was no second chance. The surgeon at the Sussex Eye Hospital sent me up to London to get a second opinion, and I saw this consultant up there, and he said, We really don't want to do it now, we like cataracts to get ripe. We'd rather wait maybe another ten years or so. I said, I just can't. He said, But as you say you're working, you've got a family, you've now got a mortgage, we'll do it, but I must point out there is a risk. I could be totally blind.

Anyway I had the op, and I was very scared, and then they took the bandages off, and I could see light, after two days this was. And then, one of the major triumphs, I went to the phone and phoned my mother, actually managed to dial the number, to tell her I could see. I don't know how thrilled she was.

Dan apparently was very emotional about it. I didn't see, he doesn't show me these things, but I heard through the grapevine, that he shed tears when he found out I was OK. But it didn't stop him bringing me a bunch of flowers, which smelled very nice, but on close examination I found it was a bunch of dandelions wrapped up in brown paper that he'd shaken aftershave over.

New world   Anyway the sight got better, and I got better. And it was fine. I mean life was really wonderful after that, we'd got the house, we had a lot of work to do, and I convalesced for about three months I think it was. But I could see better than I could see before. There were no problems. No problems at all. It was fantastic at Worcester Villas, we had so much space, if I was cheesed off, or if someone came I didn't like, I could go and sulk in another room and read a book.

Then back to work.

So far as is reasonably profitable?   I was voted as shop steward on Avent's in 1974 and that went on until I finished work over twenty years later. I was also appointed as union safety rep and I attended a union-sponsored course, a quite intensive course, on understanding and interpreting the Health & Safety at Work Act. The very first lesson showed all of us the ambiguity of the key six words: 'It shall be the duty of every employer to ensure, SO FAR AS IS REASONABLY PRACTICABLE, the health, welfare and safety at work of all his employees.' We agreed virtually unanimously that, written that way, it was a perfect let-out for employers. Because I think when you get a case that comes to court it's the lawyers that discuss, and the discussion usually comes down to semantics.

Again, every company that I've worked for, the contract of employment stated quite specifically that you were not to talk to the press or the media without prior permission and discussion with the management. So any scandal can be squashed at source. And I don't believe that legislation to protect whistle-blowers makes a lot of difference, quite honestly.

I think too many managers don't take on the responsibilities, they don't take them seriously. There should be corporate responsibility and prison sentences should be handed out. I think that would concentrate the minds of a lot of management. A company director, even if it's just the titular head of a company, if you give him a month's prison, it would definitely concentrate him on the company's safety policy and on the lower levels of employees in the company, how they work, how they're allowed to work.

Safety officers Management's attitude to safety was that at best they regarded it as a nuisance but more often than not they ignored it altogether.

I think E. W. Avent was the best company I worked for at carrying out the Health & Safety Act. Some of the others just paid lip service. They all had safety officers, they would come round the jobs and say, Oh do this, don't do that, but often when it came to some sort of issue, for example you might want a proper ladder on the job as opposed to the busted old wooden thing you'd got, and if it meant the firm had to buy one, they'd find ways round it, they'd say, Oh make do. Or, Yes we'll get you one, but it wouldn't arrive. Where health and safety clashed with cost, then cost won the day, that happened so many times.

A lot of safety officers are men who have been appointed out of the trenches, as we say. This might seem like a good idea, because if anyone should be aware of the hazards of the occupation it is the man actually doing the job who is best qualified. The reality is very different. When these men are appointed they are really grateful to get out of the trench and, rightly, consider this to be the bottom rung of the management ladder. They are usually given a smart company car and a mobile phone and can wear a smart suit and a pristine white safety helmet. Quite a contrast to

145

wallowing around covered in muck which had been their lot previously. These keen new safety officers would often choose to avoid rocking the boat and try to hold onto their promotion by turning a blind eye to the various short cuts and dangerous practices in the workplace.

A classic example of this was when we were using equipment to stop the flow of gas when carrying out modifications to live gas mains. The equipment was leaking badly and I complained, in my capacity as union-appointed safety rep and as a ganger, about the potential danger of an explosion. When I finally managed to buttonhole the company safety officer I informed him that if he didn't do something about this faulty equipment I would contact the Factory Inspectorate. He then had to inform the contracts manager of my complaint. He had heard it from me many times and was sick of hearing it, but now it was official. His reaction was furious. He instructed the safety officer to go to my job and find as many faults as possible. He found none, and nothing was done about the leaking equipment.

Back to school   After I'd been with Avent's a couple of years, British Gas insisted that gangers become qualified, and it became the rule that we had to have a certificate of competence. This meant cowboys couldn't get gangers' jobs any more, someone that bought the agent a round of drinks or two in the club couldn't get promotion on that basis. That put an end to that. I was asked by this agent, Would I be prepared to go away to school, to learn the job or whatever. I said, Yeah, of course I would. I thought, Well anything's better – especially in the winter – than mucking about in a mucky trench, sitting in a classroom being lectured. Great. Plus the fact that I did want to learn more. I did want to become skilled.

We were sent away in pairs up to a place in Norfolk called Bircham Newton. It was on an old bomber station near Kings Lynn and it was a well-known industrial school for all sorts of trades, it's still in existence now. My course was called the 'Gas Distribution Training Certificate Course on Mainlaying (Stage One) to BGC Intermediate Standard'. Most of the stuff I already knew. The only thing was you had to pass a sort of examination. And it was explained to you that, We know that the real circumstances of where you're actually working dictate that you do this a different way to what's done up here, but you will be assessed on how you do it here, according to the course. What you do when you get out of here, that's of no concern to us.

And I got my Certificate, dated 27 January 1977.

Goodbye to the Christie Sue　In August 1977, after we'd moved to Worcester Villas, in came another firm from God knows where, called A. F. Jefferies.

In most cases a new contractor paid exactly the same as I was receiving from my previous employer, but on this occasion as they'd badly underpriced the contract, the only way they could make it pay, or they thought they'd make it pay, was by paying us a lot less. I had to accept their terms and stay in the area I knew and was known in, or travel a long way outside Sussex. It was Hobson's Choice so I stayed where I was. I was expected to do the same amount of work obviously.

My money dropped by over thirty per cent overnight. By this time I'd had a good offer for the Christie Sue and sold it for three thousand quid. I got a thousand more than I'd paid for it, I'd had five years use out of it, and not spent much on it, so it wasn't a bad profit. I was planning to buy another boat. But I'd just got a mortgage for the house and the sudden drop in wages meant that in no shape or form could I take on another marine mortgage. The net result was I no longer had a boat and that was it.

The irony was that A. F. Jefferies only lasted till December 1978, and my wages then went back up again.

Allotment　By this time I'd started to rent an allotment and for a year or two I'd had the allotment as well as the boat. It probably did take up all my time but I still thought I could do both. Most of my work on the allotment was done after working hours, I got dropped off on the way home from work. I tended to spend more time on the allotment because if there's a gale blowing you can still work on your allotment, whereas you can't go to sea. So I would work on the allotment and still go over to the river every week to check the boat out.

I get my plants from the seed catalogues, grow virtually everything from seed in my shed at home, then I fetch them up here in a box on a carrier on the back of my bike. It must be the only mountain bike in the south-east of England with a carrier on the back. And it's carried literally tons of stuff from this allotment home.

I know quite a lot of other allotment holders, to various degrees of intimacy. I do like to talk, and I would say the majority of the people up here are quite left wing leaning and tend to be quite individualistic as well, which is nice.

This split chestnut fence, dividing my allotment from the path, I got from a pipeline job. It was surplus to requirements. It's getting a bit worse for wear now, but it does discourage dogs. The fencing on the right, which is horizontally laid corrugated iron, came from the Goldstone ground about eight years ago. Some guy got the demolition contract, and drove up with it. It protects the plants.

The allotment's divided almost equally into two parts, with a grass path virtually dead straight up the middle and red-and-white street-work boards making an edging. When the company changed its style of boards, these were obsolete. The ground is stony and clay-ey. But I've got two large compost heaps and every year I buy twelve to fifteen large bags. I've put literally tons and tons of compost and stuff into this ground.

I also have a device whereby I get comfrey leaves that I've grown, push them down into this fifty mil. plastic gas pipe, then drop a heavy piece of lead on top, on the end of a bit of rope. This compresses the leaves down and as they go down they rot and you get a liquid out the bottom which is pure liquid feed, and it's excellent. It smells quite rich, yes.

At the end of the path there's my shed, which I built with my sons four, five years ago. It's not very prepossessing, but by God

15. *Self-portrait with Brussels sprouts, 2001. The supports are broken galvanised steel frames for road signs.*

it's strong. The timbers holding the roof are five-by-two, you could dance on top of that. So should we get another hurricane like the one in October 1987 I don't think it would go.

From Tayberries to Swiss chard   I'll give you a tour of the allotment. On the left-hand side there's my cultivated blackberries, they're beautiful. You don't see wild blackberries weighing the branches down like that. But people were taking liberties with them. You do get to know your plants almost individually, and I saw a lot of places where they had been picked, so I put a notice up: *These berries are not growing wild. They were cultivated and paid for by the allotment holder. Please leave them alone.* I don't mind if people want to sample things like the tayberries, because they're not that common down here. But when they're filling up punnets it gets a bit saucy.

Then there's comfrey, which I use to make liquid fertilizer, globe artichoke, leeks, a mooli, they're very nice in stir-fries, Mantanghong, a winter radish, very very pale green on the outside and red on the inside, common-or-garden Webb's Wonderful cabbage lettuce, my latest sowing of spring onions, the remains of my potato patch, that's those pink fir apples, they have been excellent. Then the last knockings of peas, the second crop, they're growing up some steel reinforcing mesh that you put in concrete, very very useful, offcuts from jobs where we were doing concrete bases. Then there's your dwarf black beans, one year I grow these black ones, then I grow green, then I grow the yellow ones, Kinghorn Waxpod. Next year I might grow the three together because it does make a nice display. Then my exotic tomatoes, Green Zebra, a green striped tomato, and Black Plum, that's quite an unusual one. Last year I lost the lot with blight. I nearly cried, I was that mad.

These galvanised, three-foot long iron pipes, they used to be holding road signs, that's keeping the tayberries back. The tiny tomatoes are called something like Orange Bush, they don't grow any bigger than marbles but they're profuse, very sweet and tomatoey. Those are parsnips. I make a hole, like a post-hole, about three foot, three foot six deep, I then sieve compost and fine soil into those holes, and then plant them. And now and again I get what I think are show-bench quality parsnips, maybe two-foot-six long, perfectly straight. That's salsify, called by some people a vegetable oyster. That is a second crop of winter radish. Then scorzonera, I've grown them as an experiment, if we like 'em we'll grow 'em again, if we don't then that's that. Then winter cabbages and red cabbage which makes a nice colour in coleslaw.

Then I've got a ball cabbage which gets to be about the size of a small football, the remains of the beetroot, Swiss chard, which is like spinach but not as strong, it will crop through the winter, right round to next spring. These are winter sprouts, quite a difficult thing to grow successfully.

Tools I don't consider expensive tools a luxury, if they're good. Some of my tools I've had for years and they will last for years. Like that spade, I bought it second-hand years ago. I give it a coating of linseed oil once a year. I really do like that, the wood's beautifully smooth. What I try and do is get it rough-dug with my three sons before Christmas. In about two or three hours we can dig nearly all this allotment, especially when I'm a hundred per cent. We can get an awful lot done, when we're working in a line and having the crack and geeing each other up.

In the right-hand strip we have shallots drying and onions ripening under glass, I string 'em like the French onions sellers do and usually manage to give away one or two strings. Blackcurrant bushes, a redcurrant bush, gooseberry, strawberries, grown through special black plastic, round cucumbers, exotic tomatoes, zucchini, autumn-fruiting raspberries, some round green cucumbers called Crystal Apple, Amish Paste tomatoes, cos lettuce and sprouts, Hunter beans climbing up poles, and a French climbing bean, very nice. Then some pickling onions, Gardener's Delight tomatoes, they grow almost like bunches of grapes and they're very sweet and very prolific. Then these yellow Golden Sunrise tomatoes, the second crop of mangetout, black beans again, we hope to freeze most of these. Then beetroot, Jerusalem artichokes. Somebody gave the plants to Wendy. She did say that they're intrusive but I didn't realise they were going to be skyscrapers.

Growing excitement It has been good for me, the allotment, no doubt about it. It's outdoors and I get good vegetables. And excitement, I don't care what anybody says. It's a bit like fishing, in a way, yes. You don't know what you've got until you bring it up. And it is an achievement, I feel a certain amount of pride. It's not as good as I'd like it to be, yet. You don't think in terms of instant things, you think five years' time, with an allotment. When I worked for the market gardener, it was bloody boring quite honestly, it was short-term, it was repetitive and I wasn't getting any of the lettuces. But when you're working for yourself, it's totally absorbing. I have far shorter breaks on the allotment than I ever did at work. Maybe in another ten years I'll have got it boxed off.

And I do get an amount of isolation, I quite like that. I can be up here on my own, the gate is locked. If people want to see me they have to make the specific journey and whistle at the gate for me. Sometimes I get a bit frustrated with people. I like to talk but if I want to get on I use my walkman as a defence. People see I've got the earphones on, and I just put my hand up and say hello and they realise I'm listening to something and won't engage me in conversation.

Self-sufficiency   I would think we're ninety per cent self-sufficient in vegetables in a good year. The only thing we don't grow is maincrop spuds, because they take a lot of room. But nearly everything else. All salad stuff. In the summer if I see a tomato on the table that's not mine I want to know why.

But what that does, Wendy will spend the money she saves from vegetables on fruit: melons, grapes, bananas, oranges, whatever's in season from the supermarket that's a bit exotic. We also wouldn't be able to have some of the vegetables we do have if I didn't grow them, like mangetout, capsicums, quite expensive stuff.

We've always been great ones for making do. Money was very short and we couldn't go to the Co-op and just buy stuff. Wendy would make a lot of the children's clothes, and her own. When you see the prices the shops ask for things and Wendy would look at them and think, Well I could make something as good as that. And it was good, it was good. I'm sure if I could have made shoes she'd have had me making bloody shoes as well. Also at that particular time the jumble sales were good, this is before the antiquey collectors had moved in.

And recycling, long before the environmental thing came in. Recycling is mainly down to Wendy. She's always recycled tins, rinses the tins out, crushes them, that's how good she is. Well, I made the crusher.

I suppose we've always improvised. Obviously for the last I don't know how many years people have been becoming aware of natural resources, they are finite, but we did it mainly because it was expedient. I would see something and say, Hello that would be useful. A classic of that is the wooden sailing blocks I bought from a boatbuilder. I kept them for ages and in the end, when we had to move a heavy press to a basement in north-west London, I used it. If I've got a problem, I'll find a way, with some ingenuity, of getting over it.

We did recycle beer bottles because we used to brew our own. So we'd obviously buy crown caps and a cap thing and keep all our bottles. Christ, we had some good nights on that. When we lived at New Steine I'd walk down, cross the road, go shrimping, get a load of shrimps and bring a plate of shrimps back, and then fresh bread and butter and a pile of shrimps and a couple of pints of home brew, that was really good. I wouldn't take shrimps from there now, if they are there, but then it was fine. Yeah I liked that.

Not if I have to   Anyway, to go back to Jefferies. I was never happy working for that firm. I didn't get on with the director at all and he didn't like me because I refused to be a navvy. He came on the site with his manager when I happened to be lending a hand with the digging and asked how many pipes a day we were putting in. I told him. He said, Well I want one pipe for every man, every man's got to dig a pipe. I said, Well I'm not going to. He said, Well you're digging now. I said, Yeah, but the minute I've got to, I'm not going to, I'm not going to, I'm a ganger. And leaped out of the trench. He couldn't handle this, he thought I was a lunatic.

Fumes & filters   Another incident, two guys on the job were carrying out a process called encapsulation, it involved grit-blasting round a joint that had a leak. They had a complete helmet to protect them from the flying grit. And the air they were breathing inside the helmet was blown via a filter from the compressor that also powered the grit-blaster.

And one of these guys, I'd known them for years, Roger Bradford, he rang me up one night and he said, We're having trouble with these new filters, Peter, they couldn't get the normal filters for us when we wanted a new stock of filters, and we think we can smell engine oil in the helmet. So I rang Antonia's father, who was a doctor, and asked him about hot or warm engine oil fumes. And he said, They are carcinogenic, and in concentrated form they are very dangerous.

So as the safety rep and shop steward I then contacted the contracts manager and said, Could they please get the proper filters for the men because they're getting fumes in the helmet which are carcinogenic. And he said, Oh we're having a problem getting these filters, the new ones we're getting are supposed to be OK but I'll see what I can do. So then I think another week went past and there's still no news of these filters.

So then I rang the filter company, I said, Do you have such-and-such filters in stock? He said, Yes. I said, Have you had an order recently from the company I work for – I explained who I was – to renew their supply? He said, No, we used to have a regular order, but we can't understand why they haven't re-ordered them. He said, We've never been out of stock.

The following day I went in and saw the contracts manager and I said, Right, you know I've been onto you about the filters? He said, Yes, we can't get hold of them. I said, You're a fucking liar, mister. Because I know you have not tried to get those filters, there is no shortage of those filters, we're talking about saving pennies at the expense of men's bloody lives.

He said, Who do you think you are, coming in here giving me all this? I said, I think I'm the safety rep and shop steward on this contract, and I've checked up, I know damn well you haven't ordered this stuff. You get those filters within two days, or I'm going to have the Health and Safety inspector in and shut down that process.

Anyway, whatever the truth of it was, they got the filters. This was November 1977. I still have the notes I took at the time.

Goodbye A. F. Jefferies   Jefferies were losing money hand over fist. And there was an awful lot of slanging to and fro between us and the management and the owner of the company. But in the end I asked the managing director, I said, Well if you carry out this contract according to British Gas's code of practice, can you make a profit? He said, It's absolutely out of the question. I said, Well then you've condemned yourself out of your own mouth, you've proved that you did not price the contract correctly, because if you price a contract to make a profit, then you must expect to do everything to the letter of the law, especially when there are so many safety aspects to do with gas. You've got to base your profit on doing the job absolutely to spec.

It wasn't long after this, in December 1978, that they did pull out of the contract, in spite of paying poor wages, and William Press came in.

Hello William Press   So it was Goodbye Jefferies, which I wasn't sorry to see the back of, and Hello William Press, which at the time had quite a formidable reputation. It was an old-established company, a big organisation. I can't say that it was a family company but it was started by a guy called William Press. It was the big company in the South of England. So this was the business, the real McCoy.

But we still had quite a lot of problems with the management. Unfortunately in construction and civil engineering they're still in the Victorian era as far as their thinking's concerned, and do like to hire and fire people just like that.

But the actual structure of William Press was quite good and their back-up, meaning the plant and their resources, were good. If you wanted four cranes on a job on a Monday, they could get you four cranes there.

Power game   I did five years on Press's, from 1978 to 1983, did quite a few big jobs. Like laying a major new pipeline across East-bourne Golf Course in 1980. Incidentally I think the story of how I got on that job is pertinent. A ganger's wages did vary according to the particular contract and at the time I wasn't earning much, and getting fed up with the work. Then I was offered work by another contractor, Moxom's, that had part of the Sussex contract, and they were paying good money. Maybe they could afford it because they weren't too top-heavy on the management side. My mate Dan was working on it. And I was offered a start on this company.

But Mr Kay, who was the District Engineer of Brighton, came to see me. He said, I hear you're thinking of changing your job. I said, Yes. He said, Well I'm not going to allow it. I said, You're what, you're not my employer. He said, No but I dictate what work you do, and if you go on for Moxom's in this area I'll see what work you do, and it won't be the sort of work you can earn any-thing on. So that was that. I said, Well sod you, that's literally what I said, I'm not putting up with this, it's up to me to sell my labour where I want to. So then Press's transferred me over to this job on Eastbourne Golf Course, where I was running two gangs at the same time. So I was moved out of the Brighton area, totally.

I don't know if Kay was trying to bully me, but he liked having me handy for doing the quality of work that he wanted. But that's the sort of power those people have. But he lost out, because I did move. All right I didn't go on to the firm that I wanted, but I was moved out of the area, I wasn't doing work for him. I was working under another man called Laurie Robinson who was District Engineer in Eastbourne.

One of a handful   William Press is a universal company, they do work in a lot of other countries. I did apply at one point to get work with them in Egypt, and went up to Darlington for the test and the interview. My technical ability was OK and the references I had from the district engineers were absolutely excellent, like this one from Laurie Robinson:

> *I have had first hand knowledge of the workmanship of Mr Richards for the last nine years ... He has shown himself to be capable of the complete range of mainlaying skills from organising Iris Stop operations to running lead joints.*
>
> *He has a good knowledge of contract documents; is aware of his statutory obligations under PUSWA and HASWA and has excellent control of his team members.*
>
> *He has always achieved good productivity and is one of a handful of contract mainlayers all the District Engineers of my acquaintance seek to employ when a task arises which is particularly difficult.*
>
> *It has always been my wish for the contractor to employ Mr Richards in this district and it has always been with great reluctance that I have occasionally had to agree to him leaving for more important work elsewhere.*

They said, These are the best references we've seen. But I got the knock-back. They didn't give a reason but quite frankly I don't think they wanted a busy shop steward out in Egypt.

Then in the late eighties I tried to get on the gas in New Zealand. It was a really fantastic project, the whole of New Zealand going on mains gas as opposed to bottled gas, and I wrote to the guy that was in charge. And he wrote back and said that he would give my application to the company that was carrying out the work. It was Press International. So it goes without saying, I got the knock-back again.

Stone removal   Towards the end of my time with William Press I developed renal colic. This was in 1982. It was not funny. I was sitting in the kitchen one Sunday morning and I had a pain in my back. I thought, Oh, must have been shovelling awkward yesterday or something. Anyway the pain got worse and then eventually I went to the bedroom and I was kneeling on the floor and it was that bad I couldn't even swear. It was so bad. So my son has seen me, and I've gone ashen, and he's rang the doctor.

And he sent me for tests at Hove General and everything on the Monday. I had X-rays and all the rest of it, and they came to the conclusion, Yes I've got a kidney stone. And they said, It's too big to pass, it'll have to be removed surgically. So they made an appointment for me to see a consultant at Hove General, and it was some months after this that I actually went in. But I didn't get another dose of that renal colic at all.

Dressing down   The operation was OK and afterwards I could get up and have a shave and everything. I refused to use a bedpan, I didn't want any of that nonsense, I don't mind peeing in a bottle, but the other thing, I just couldn't envisage myself doing that.

And one of the doctors, I think she was called the Houseman, she gave me a real dressing down. She was a bit of tyrant. Someone had lent me a paperback, called *The Abuse of Power*, and I used to leave this out on my bed, very ostentatiously, whenever this woman came round.

And I convalesced for about four or five months. But I could feel that for up to a year afterwards. That was that episode.

The Wenroc contract   William Press were in the contract for five years, and then Wenroc Ltd came in for two years, in 1983. The most significant thing about working for these people was that after a year they were in the hands of the official receiver. We were told that our money would be OK and we'd carry on working as per normal. But then they said the company had been taken over by another company, and it would be a new employment.

What they proposed was, sacking us on Friday, but we'd be taking home the vans, coming back to the same job, with the 'new' company, on the Monday, and not calling it continuous employment. So that means we're new employees with no rights whatsoever, no right of appeal, no right to a fair wage structure, and God knows what else. And no redundancy at the end of the expected contract. I thought, Well I'm not having this, and appealed to the Industrial Tribunal.

Tribunal   On the first day of the hearing my so-called union organiser buggered off to Croydon. So I had no back-up when I argued our case. I was not very happy.

I pointed out that I'd done a search at Company House (at my own expense), and that the 'new' company, that we were allegedly working for on the Monday, didn't exist till the following Friday. The Chairman dismissed this, said it was just a technicality. And that was it. The whole thing was technicalities. Result was, I lost the case.

United we sit   Some months later I saw this same union guy sitting in our office, in our depot, at Cowfold. I remember it was a really cold, bleak January, one of those cutting days, and I'd had a bad day, and there was this union guy, well overweight, sitting in the manager's office with his feet up drinking a cup of coffee.

This guy said, Oh I understand you've been making complaints about me. I said, Yes, you really dropped me in it. I said, You're sitting there, you've got your fat body in a suit that I paid for, you've just got out of the comfortable car that I've paid for, and you're sitting there ... And at this point he said, Don't get excited, don't get excited. I said, I'm not excited Jim, All the time I'm naming you, I'm calling you something, you're safe. The minute I've run out of words to say, I said, that's the time when you've got to be scared, because I'm sick of you.

I said, I expect it from the sort of shit like this, pointing at the manager, I expect that, that's part of the game, but not you, you're on our side, allegedly. And with that I just stormed out the office. I came very close to doing something I would have been sorry for. Well I wouldn't have been sorry, but I'd have been punished for it afterwards, so I left it at that.

I didn't lose faith in the union. Because I think a lot of what's wrong with unions is that the lay people don't take enough interest, they're complacent. Then the minute something goes wrong they want Boyd QC in there doing it for them. So anyway that was that little episode, that was very important.

Collective? We never got collective back-up, you can get it if you can get fifty people together in a canteen and harangue them and appeal to their better nature or whatever, but you can't do it with a scattered labour force that are all getting different pay. For example a ganger on a job where they earn good money – and some of them did earn good money – there's no way you're going to get him to back up anybody else.

Some unions may be more helpful than others but a lot of it's down to individuals. The system is such that you get regional organisers that are virtually a law unto themselves. It depends on what they're like as to how good the union treatment is. If you're a union official and there's nothing going on you're getting an easy ride. They only have to earn their money when the men are actually out and they've got to negotiate some sort of settlement, that's when they have to work. But the union structure is such that you can't get rid of incompetent officials. You can't.

Shop steward As shop steward I was representing up to forty or fifty men on the Sussex gas contract. Not everybody joined the union. It wasn't a closed shop. I like the idea of a closed shop, but it wasn't. I was representing the union members on the contract, several gangs, but not necessarily in touch with each other. If you've got a workforce that's split up across quite a large county like Sussex, it's very difficult to maintain communication.

My union duties mainly depended on people phoning me. In this sort of work the lorry-drivers are the grapevine. You learn what happens through them, from gang to gang, they carry the stories. Often they're changed a bit.

At this time I did go away to union school for an induction course. And it was very nice to meet other shop stewards from other walks of life, and other jobs. Really nice, I really enjoyed that. The people had the same sort of objects, and attitudes, as yourself.

16. *Supporting the ambulance strike, Crawley Ambulance Station, late 1980s.*

Management   As a shop steward you're not helped or assisted by the management. I won't say they stopped you, but they don't do anything constructive.

An interesting time on Press's, which is a big company, was when we had a particularly nasty line manager. We'd have a quarterly regional meeting with upper management, very important sort of people. But he would want a pre-meeting meeting at Hassocks to discuss local issues. He said, We don't want to bother the big noises with all these little parochial things. He wanted to get stuff out the way that could be embarrassing to him, and spike my guns, before they could be used at the meeting with the big boys.

So what I did, I prepared an agenda for the local meeting, but it was totally different to what I had to say in front of the big boys at the quarterly meeting. And he got very nasty about this. He gave me an awful lot of abuse without any witnesses afterwards. And I just said to him, Well George, what do you think I just got off, a banana boat, or the Fishguard ferry? I know what your game is.

Who gives a damn?   I saw an article in the *Independent*, 'Who gives a damn about the working man?' The sad truth is the working man doesn't give a damn about the working man, at least that is my experience. All the time things are going along OK they don't bother to attend meetings. The only time there was any hint of solidarity was when there was a crisis, and then it was too little too late. Even when there was trouble on the horizon only a hand-ful of members turned up to meetings.

A lot of them are like closet tories inasmuch as the only thing they see wrong with wealth and power is that it's someone else who's got it, not them. 'The working class can kiss my arse / I've got the coddie's – or the foreman's – job at last.' They don't ever see further than this week's bonus or next week's pay packet. Very very few have the integrity to look ahead and see what's going to be best for everybody.

I don't think for one minute that I'm any different, except that I see that in the long run if we all pull together it's better for me as an individual. It's not necessarily through altruism, I just know that in the end it benefits me if we all stick together.

The few minor triumphs I did achieve were by using what little knowledge I've got of industrial law or by fighting as dirty as the managements in my industry, and never, I repeat never, by solidarity of the membership.

I often envy the comradeship that a lot of working men in the old industrial areas share even when unemployed. No such feeling here. Perhaps the reason for this is that there is no one major industry, and never has been, to unify or weld the men and women together in collective hardship or adversity.

Step up or shut up   On many occasions I was a real pain in the arse to my employers, once I had been elected as a shop steward and safety rep. On one occasion shortly after my new employer had started the contract his chief agent approached me and offered me a supervisor's position and was most surprised when I turned it down. I would have been flattered if I had been offered the job because they thought I would make a good supervisor, but I was under no illusion that this was a shut-up offer. My reputation must have gone before me.

This was about the same time that we'd had the dispute over the Wenroc contract and I had made very strong criticisms at the local branch office of the union about the full-time official. They did not want to rock the union boat by making a formal complaint to Headquarters. When I stated that I had no such reservations they started making noises to the effect that I might like to go to Ruskin College.

I couldn't fail to draw a parallel between the two situations.

Full circle   After Wenroc, I then went and worked for J Murphy's, who got the Sussex contract. This was 1986, unfortunately they only had it for one year. I liked Murphy's, they were a good firm. They weren't picky, they paid reasonably well, and I particularly got on well with the main agent, a guy called Pat Powers who was an Irishman. And after I'd left Murphy's, or they'd lost the contract in Sussex, he rang me and told me if I felt like a change I'd always get a job with him. They were my favourite firm.

Murphy's were undercut in their bid for the contract by Press, and Press was back in again from 1986 to 1989. But it was a different Press, it was a Press that had been bought out by Fairclough, a totally different firm, not such a good one.

Then Mainline came in for one-and-a-half years, a Yorkshire firm. I wasn't impressed. We had lots of trouble with them because they thought they were going to pay Yorkshire money to soft Southerners and we wouldn't buy it. And I did find out from experience with their management, which was nearly all Yorkshire, that Yorkshire people like plain speaking when they're dishing it out, but they didn't like to be on the receiving end very much. And I managed to get the status quo going back the other way very quickly. They only lasted one and a half years.

And then in 1990 O. C. Summers came back in. And this is like full circle because the first firm I worked for as a pieceworker, nearly thirty-odd years earlier, was Summers.

Last seven years   After 1990 OCS lost the the Sussex gas contract and moved out of Sussex. It was another Hobson's Choice. The incoming contractor was offering self-employment and no guaranteed minimum wage. No way was I going to accept that. So I had to move to the OCS Croydon-based contract covering South London from Kent to Epsom, which involved long drives to work and a lot of stress.

I did seven years with OCS.

In January 1997 I started experiencing severe pains in my chest. After an ECG, a blood test and a chest X-ray I saw a cardiologist at the Sussex County who thought my chest pains were neuralgia or heartburn! But he arranged for me to do the treadmill test some time in the future.

On 20 February I went to work, had two very severe attacks and came home at 2 o'clock. The doctor advised me not to go back to work until I had taken the treadmill test. In March I took the test and also heard that the ECG indicated some furring up of the arteries. On 25 April I had an angiogram at the Sussex County and was told I would have to have a triple bypass.

After six months on statutory sick pay the date of the operation was still uncertain and OCS dismissed me in August 1997. On 4 September I received the minimum tax-free £2,205 statutory redundancy pay. The way they treated me over all this prompted me to write a letter to the Chairman of Laing, the parent company, in which I let off a bit of steam.

On 14 January 1998 I had a *quadruple* bypass. On 2 April I started cardiac rehab and on 7 April Nick and I began work on this book.

LOOKING BACK

Fitness　Manual workers get plenty of exercise without going to health clubs. Mind you, the type of physical work we do is not exactly designed to benefit you physically or mentally, to put it mildly. If you're not fit you can easily do yourself an injury. I remain quite supple in my back and particularly in my abdominal muscles because of the exercises I do at home. But some of it is vanity, I mean I only weigh just over eleven stone now and I feel better if I'm like that.

Stress　You don't hear much about the stress suffered by manual workers but I am convinced my heart condition was stress-related. I packed in the roll-ups and the huge fried breakfasts donkey's years ago. I'm not into that particular mode of self-destruction.

When I worked at Barton Court, we used to grind our own pigmeal in a hammer mill fixed to the power take-off of a tractor. This is unbelievably noisy and it went on for three or four hours. That was stressful. But I wasn't really aware of stress at work in the early years because it was all a novelty. I think when I first became aware of stress was when we worked on these radar towers, two hundred and twenty feet up.

Money worries　As a married labourer I found piecework stressful inasmuch that, say if it was raining so hard you couldn't work on Monday and Tuesday, you were sweating blood that you'd be able to tear into it and earn a week's wages on Wednesday, Thursday and Friday. And quite often we didn't. And it did seem very unjust to me that even if we didn't work Monday and Tuesday we'd be out there sitting in the shed waiting to dive out and try and do something. There was a desperation about it sometimes.

That was stress because I was worried about my family. When I first started as a labourer, I was quite happy to be broke on Saturday night, it didn't bother me that much, I expected to have no money in my pocket. If I had enough to buy half an ounce of Old Holborn every couple of days, that was enough. Or we could get a sub. I borrowed far more money when I was single than I ever did when I was married.

Pneumatic drill   But I really started becoming aware of stress at work when I started working on gas mains, and using a pneumatic drill. Again, in the early days, and for quite a lot of my working life, ear-muffs, face-masks and that sort of thing, were not statutory, we didn't have them. And sometimes, on some of the jobs, the noise went on for weeks and weeks.

Like laying the new main down St James Street, which was a concrete road, and it was just days and days of breaking up concrete with a jack-hammer.

The labourers on that job were not paid at piece-rate, they were paid a daily rate and they were given an extra day's money as compensation because of the type of job it was. And I think I went through eight or ten different labourers there. They just couldn't stand it, and these are tough Irish guys that are used to this sort of work. It was consistent concrete, and it was a narrow street and the sound reverberated from side to side off the shop windows or whatever.

Which is why I got rather upset with a shopkeeper down there that said, How much longer is that row going on, it's giving me a headache? And when I said, Well, how do you think we feel? he said, You're used to it. My reply was, If you got a slap in the head every day of the week, would you be used to it by Saturday night? Which he didn't appreciate I don't think, but I mean that's what it was like, that was very stressful.

In your face   And another thing that was very stressful in St James Street was the amount of traffic right beside your face. You had buses going up there, and our faces when we were in the trench – I actually measured it – were eighteen inches from the bus exhausts. They were that close. The ironic thing was that when I spoke to a bus inspector, we were halfway through that job, he said, Well, these buses could have all been diverted up Edward Street and down the sea-front. You didn't need to have it. There were seven bus-routes going up there at the time. He said, It could have been arranged, but no one contacted us. Oh well. Again, it seems like we're just a disposable form of labour or whatever and no one's really considered it.

The St James Street set-up is about as bad as it gets. All the time you've got to be on your guard, to watch what this person does, what that person does. When your lorry comes on the job to clear up, make sure he's not blocking the road for too long, or if you get a motorist that's getting particularly awkward, you've got to try and keep him quiet. I didn't use the aggressive approach all the time. Sometimes I would snap when people were being particularly stupid, and insisting that they have a right of way even though it's only going to be five minutes.

17. The Man, or just an extension of a shovel?

Centre-stage Another stressful time was when we were doing the conversion to natural gas and we were putting these big section valves in. I was really thrown in at the deep end. It was a job in Southwick and it involved cutting out a large section of twelve-inch diameter pipe, and two valves going in. I'd never done this operation before, it was the first one in our sector, and everyone was going to be there. When I say everyone I mean the people from our firm, the management people and all sorts of engineers on SEGAS. And I was very much centre-stage. This is at night.

And I didn't sleep properly for two nights prior to the job because I was that worried about it. The crucial thing is the measurement. You've cut the section out of the main, and they're going to put these various components in there, different valves and things, and if it doesn't fit ... We're talking about half-inch tolerance maximum, either end. If you haven't got it right, it's all wrong, then it's really embarrassing, it causes a lot of trouble. And I was very nervous that night. I had quite a few men with me, because I had another one or two gangs, but I was the man in charge. Not overall charge, obviously, there were engineers on the site.

That was three days, and nights, of real tension. The engineer and everybody comes round afterwards and says, Oh a good job, nice job, and well done to your crew. Which is nice. But I was the key man.

Indispensable?   The way my work has dictated so much of my life was driven home that time in 1974 when Wendy had taken the kids to visit our friends in Shrewsbury, and I couldn't go with them because I was doing quite a major job by Hove Cemetery. We were diverting a main and there was quite a lot of men involved on the job, including a crane, machines and a welder. The job had reached a crucial stage, and I really couldn't be missed. I'd stuck with it through a lot of the bad bits and I thought, Well I'd better stick with it now. Which is why I was around the Bank Holiday Dan got me into trouble at the Seven Stars.

Another time I felt I couldn't be spared from work was the time I had that renal colic, in 1982. I'd been moved down to another big job in Shoreham, twenty-four inch major, doubling up with another gang. I was brought in as I had quite a lot of experience of large-diameter pipework, and there was a certain amount of prestige – no extra money – attached to this kind of job. I had four or five men on, at that particular time. I worked right up to the day before I went into hospital, which was good.

Migraines   The pressure of time was always there, always. Especially over the last few years. I used to get migraines, but I haven't had one since I stopped work. They were awful. I was averaging one or two a week up till just before I finished work. I've had them last for a day, and I've had a two-day job before now. When I had two or three guys with me, I'd sometimes go and lay in the van on my own, for an hour, and they'd go. But when it was down to two of us, I just couldn't do that. It affected my eyes first, then I would feel nausea and also diarrhoea. Light became very painful, and my vision was restricted. I took migraleve but they didn't do the job. The circumstances we were working in were not conducive to carrying medication, or even being aware of when one was coming on, or I might be in the middle of doing something quite tricky when it came on. People think it's just me being a prima donna, but if you've got a migraine and you're working with or near a pneumatic drill, it is very very painful. And it made me very bad-tempered. I managed not to really take it out on any-body, but there were lots of times when I would just like to have walked away from the job. Some of the other guys knew about it, and they were OK.

Awkward squad   On the St James Street job, where the guys were getting paid an extra day a week, we were doing a road crossing at Rock Gardens on a Saturday night. I hadn't been well, I thought maybe I was coming down with flu. And it was raining like hell. And these two Irish lads working with me didn't show up. So my-self and the jointer had to do the job and I got soaked and I wasn't at all happy.

On the Monday when they came I said, Where the hell were you two Saturday night? You told me you'd work, you didn't show up. If you didn't want to work I could have got someone else. So I said, The extra shift you get for the week, I'm going to make sure you don't get that. And on the Friday the jointer that was work-ing with me, another Irish guy, said, One of them, the big fellow, he's going to have you. He's going to jack today and he's going to have you.

So for that day I just walked around with a road-pin, which is about a four-foot long iron bar. I didn't have it out of my hands all day, I thought, Well if you do start, Tom, you're not going to walk over me. But he didn't do anything. I see the guy now, and he's worked with me since, and it's OK, but at that time there was a lot of muttering and there again, they were talking in Gaelic, these two. They could have been talking about the football or the weather, but when you know that atmosphere is there you natu-rally assume they're on about how they're going to do you, sort of thing. That was quite stressful, to put it mildly. I knew what they were capable of.

To boil it right down to a single thing, I think that what I've had to do over the years is, I've tried to do, and had to do, a skilled job for the most part using unskilled labour.

The Public   As a ganger my first duty is the public, not the firm's profit. That's what we're told when we qualify: You are on public works, there are many priorities, but that is your first. You must never lose sight of that. And the public can be fairly awkward.

On one job, in a residential street, this group of women are coming along the road, they've obviously been to some meeting. And this woman said to me, My goodness, what a mess! And I was very fussy about pedestrian footways and the public on my jobs. Oh, I said, I don't think it's much of a mess, madam. For the sake of the convenience of pressing a button and getting cooking, or comfort, or whatever, it's a very small price to pay. I said, How would you like to be like some poor old woman, squatting over a charcoal fire in a mud hut? At this she sort of snorted and walked away. So oh dear, I'm in hot water again. My mouth.

The next day we were in full swing, the two guns going, the digger going, loading the lorry, blah blah blah. And this other woman came out from one of the houses down the end. She said, How much longer is this noise going to go on? I said, Well, till five o'clock, lady, what's your problem? She said, Well my father's very ill, the doctor says he won't last the night and we'd like him to go peacefully. I said, Well I don't really have the authority to shut the job down, but I will shut it down, that's it. And I did. About two o'clock, I shut it down. The next day, she came out, she said, Thank you very much, my father did die during the night, and we're very grateful to you for doing what you did. And I think there was a public Thank-you in the *Argus* at the end of that week.

Which was quite good. It didn't give me any medals, but I think cancelled out my bit of lip to the first woman. And in any case, if ever we're approached by someone like that, in a perfectly polite way, we'd always co-operate if it's possible. Whether it's moving a machine, moving pipes or doing something for people. Nearly every gang that you meet will do this, if they're approached the right way.

Buffer zone   None of these problems ever get above the gangerman. He's in the front line. The agent doesn't deal with any of that. And when it's coming down the other way, when I get a ticking off about things that are done or not done on the job, the lads don't get that, even though sometimes it's their fault. It always comes back to you. The nearest I can equate to it, it's like NCOs in the army. They're in between and, apart from your ability, you're there as a buffer, to take stick from both sides as it were.

Being a ganger you're in a situation of dichotomy. On the one hand you are obviously not management, because you look like one of the labourers that are working with you, for the most part you dress the same. On the other hand you've got the responsibility of the whole job. But it's played down by your employers all the time. And that's it, on the one hand it's played down, but on the other hand you're very aware that you are The Man, the key figure, that if there's a problem on the job, the police, the public, the management, the engineers, will come and see you, put the finger on you. On the one hand you're an extension of a shovel, especially nowadays where the gangs are so small, but on the other hand you've still got all the legal obligations and responsibilities.

Always on the edge I never got complacent, I never got complacent about the safety aspect of things, say about being in a trench with a certain depth. I'd take chances myself in quite deep holes, but I wouldn't expect anybody else to.

When I was on a new job I could never relax, even though it might be an operation I'd done quite a few times. Every site is different. It's a perverted way of thinking, but I thought, Well if I ever get that confident, then things will go wrong. So therefore I was always on edge. Not entirely self-induced, but maybe there was a little bit of that in it. I reckoned if I thought about the worst that could happen, then it wouldn't happen.

18. Redkiln Roundabout, Horsham, 6 August 1987. Peter manages machinery on the lorry. Thirteen days later Pappy (right) nearly had a finger taken off by one of these pipes as it was lowered into a trench.

Progress for who?   There's definitely been a revolution in mainlaying in the last thirty years. I mean at one time, even in my time in Brighton, you would see twenty, thirty men in a gang digging up the street and laying these massive electric cables. You just don't see that now. As I say, the job is more mechanised. Different methods of doing the same sort of work, you've got machines that can bore underground like a mole and take cables with them, and that sort of thing. There's less need for hard physical labour and what there is has become more skilled. Virtually any part of that job, if you work in the street, you have to have qualifications.

In the nineties, when I was based in Croydon, we experienced what is often wryly referred to as progress, which means that for the people in the trenches things got worse. As the contracts changed, so my gang got less and less. Eventually, there was just three of us. And later on I was down to two, which in my opinion, for the work we were doing and the size of the stuff we were handling, was totally inadequate and unsafe. It wasn't right.

But at the same time some of the conditions you work in are just as bad as they were forty or fifty years ago. That's why I think the job has got very very bad, that's why it's gone sour. The sort of cliché you hear now is, Oh the job's got serious. Gangers have got more responsibilities now than they used to have. But it's always been serious. What's happened now is that there is no kudos, no status, attached to being a ganger.

Before I left the industry all sorts of petty restrictions were starting to come in, all sorts of things that as far I can say boiled down to image. You will wear a hard hat, you will wear a safety vest, you will wear this. But at the same time they didn't introduce things like pneumatic drills that take a lot of the shock and vibration out, which have been around for twenty or thirty years, because that cost a lot of money. A safety vest is a few bob, those helmets were the cheapest they could buy, the same with the earmuffs. But anything that could really make the job better in terms of noise, vibration, dust, that never happened. And that's what I'm really cynical about, the whole image thing.

They allege that you're using plastic pipe now instead of iron, so therefore you don't need as many hands. But if you're working in deep excavations, and if everybody – everybody! all two of you – are down there, and something goes wrong, you've got no chance, no chance at all.

Well I'm out of it now, but I think it's sad. And I think it's wrong, because wealths of experience are being thrown away. I mean I could still be useful, I'm sure. I could be handing on what I've learned over all these years.

Reflection   I do reflect about myself, but with a time lapse.

The things that are painful or the few occasions I have felt remorse are left alone until a suitable amount of time has removed the sharp edge of the memories. I feel remorse only where I have hurt those who are near and dear to me even though at the time I felt justified in taking courses of action that by most people's standards were extreme.

As for the people outside my close circle who have received verbal or physical reactions from me, I have not one iota of regret. I felt and feel they deserved everything that happened to them and in some cases a lot more than they got.

The good times are brought to mind quite often and quite deliberately, perhaps as some sort of latent therapy. For example when we moved into the garden basement flat at New Steine after living in cramped conditions at Devonshire Place, although most people's idea of space and freedom is certainly not a one-bedroom basement flat with two adults and two kids. But everything is relative.

Commitment   I have always been very cautious about committing myself to relationships. Wendy was the exception and I have been very fortunate in my married life, some would say more than I deserve.

Her attributes are legion. She has run the home for many years in very difficult circumstances, she was a good mother and is now a good friend to our three sons. She has put up with me and all the baggage I carry.

She has never had a lot of money to spend on clothes but has always looked smart and fashionable on the outside and always catered for my taste in what you don't see. And what is most important I fancy her rotten. I don't know when love changed but over the many years that we have been together it has gone from the mad, passionate 'can't bear to be away from you for a moment' to something more profound and strangely more tactile, for example if one of us leaves the house we always kiss goodbye.

19. Portrait of Wendy by Peter.

As far as the tactile side of things is concerned I once asked Wendy which was the most important, sex or cuddles? She couldn't decide, and as we have had an electric blanket for some time now it's not just a question of me giving her my warmth and her giving me her cold as it used to be in the good old days.

We have had some very bad patches in the past (most of them my fault) but I am very happy to say we have weathered them and come out all the stronger. We seldom allow an argument to stretch over a couple of days and sometimes when it has been me in the wrong I break the ice by saying 'I'm ready to accept your apology now'. I don't always get away with it but it's worth a try.

When I think back over the past I can't for the life of me imagine life without her. The fishing, the allotment, the photography, my attempt at writing a novel, would all have seemed pointless without her. There is no logic behind this unless it has been that she has given me a sense of security over the years and never shot me down in flames as my parents did.

I am so glad that we have each other and I feel if Wendy is with me I can handle anything that life can throw at me.

Getting ahead   I do not believe my life would have been a lot different unless outside influences over which I had no control had come into play. Many friends have suggested that with my intelligence my life could have been much easier. I don't know if I am intelligent, I do know I can give a very convincing impression of being bright. But whatever my IQ is I have never felt inferior to anyone. I know there are people who are better looking, better read etcetera, but these have never made me feel uncomfortable nor do they automatically get my respect.

Very early on in our married life we had the idea of emigrating to Canada. We thought we wouldn't get anywhere much here, just being prepared to keep your head down, go to work every day and do as you're told. Things were stacked against you.

I know people would argue that they got on, did this and achieved that. Well some people do, I've got friends that have. Perhaps it's my personality, that I won't play the political game, small 'p', and I'm not ruthless and nasty enough, maybe. Well I'm nasty enough, but I'm not nasty enough to get on professionally. So that's really what gave us the idea of trying to emigrate.

Also we didn't feel that we had really strong ties here. As far as my family was concerned I wouldn't have hesitated to get on a boat or a plane and go somewhere. As I've said, I applied for work with William Press International in Egypt, and later New Zealand, but I was turned down. I'd been a thorn in the flesh of the management at home.

Nowadays we couldn't just up and go. If we won the lottery and someone said, Oh you can move to a nice warmer climate, I don't think we could. We've got too many friends, too many people here. We'd have to move everybody en masse to wherever we were going.

Another life? But I suppose I could have lived another kind of life, yes.

I always have been really fascinated by dance. Still am. I do like rhythm and I do like movement. And when I was at boarding school I had a girlfriend, briefly, who could tap-dance, a very naughty girl, who was always in trouble, and I did have a few tap lessons from her. I don't know if I've mentioned that to anybody for years. I was only about nine or ten at the time.

But even now I do like watching virtually all the dance programmes, classical ballet, but particularly flamenco, and modern dance. Very much so. I saw a video of *Carmen*, but performed as a flamenco, some years ago, that was very exciting.

And I quite like the big American musicals. A lot of the stories are crappy, but some of the dancing, the choreography, was fantastic. Not so much *West Side Story*, more Ken Russell's *The Boyfriend*. I must confess that when I saw that I was in a very strange state, inasmuch that it was the first time I ever did an acid trip, but I really did like that, that was wonderful, stoned or straight.

As for playing a musical instrument, yes, I did have piano lessons at boarding school but I didn't apply myself as assiduously as I should have done. Later on when I was in the ATC I played what's called a cavalry trumpet in our band and I did enjoy it and got quite good at it. Again I didn't really pursue that after I came out of the ATC but I think I could have done, and have been reasonably accomplished.

Those ambitions were more in my mind, or the front of my mind, than being a train driver or a paratrooper for example, I did have those sort of leanings. I think if I had thought that my ability matched my ambition, I probably would have gone down one of those roads, but I never did. They were just fantasies. But one never knows, maybe given different circumstances I would have pursued one of them.

Seafarer? When I was working for Mr Nye in Shoreham, someone said that if I went up to Hull he'd give me an introduction to a skipper and I'd get a berth on one of the trawlers. But in a way I'm glad that I didn't, because the life of people on those East Coast deep-sea trawlers, even in my lifetime, is very very hard.

I played at fishing, not to put too fine a point on it. I suppose it would have been all right if I'd found the right guy to work with me. If I could have made a reasonable living, if I could have made wages plus, then I think I would have done. It is a bit of a gamble. And the romance would very soon wear off. But I quite liked it because it was totally different, and I still am fascinated by the sea, I never walk past any port anywhere without having a look over the side and see what's floating. Some people say I'd look to see what's floating on a duck-pond, which I probably would.

Occupations, preoccupations   Am I an obsessive person? No, but people that have worked with me would say that I am, inasmuch that I like things done properly. For the job's sake, not for my employer's sake, for my own sake.

I do like gadgets, I must admit, and if I had a great deal more income, my house would be full. I see this particular gadget, I've not dreamt of doing what the thing's function is, and immediately try and think of jobs to do with it.

The model-building ties in with my thing with the sea. I do like ships and I do like sailing boats. They're just nice things to have. It's like a functional ornament, whereas Wendy would fill the place up with art deco stuff if she could afford it.

Photography   And I've collected quite a lot of photography paraphernalia. I like images, particularly of people. A lot of people assumed that I would go on to video but I'm not interested in moving images. I like the frozen moment. Landscapes, and again, boats. I like photographing boats in harbour and harbour scenes, that sort of thing. And children, after a bit they get bored with playing up to the camera, and then you can get some reasonable shots of them. Particularly Lou's nine kids, when his lot were young they were a handful but they were very photogenic.

Knives and guns   I like knives, particularly folding knives. Again it's that functional thing. I'm not particularly interested in daggers and swords, a knife is a tool. I do like knives. I've quite a variety. I get quite, not upset exactly, but a bit peeved, if I lose a knife. I lost one with what's called a hawksbill which is a curved blade, up the allotment two years ago and I keep hoping I'm going to dig it up. I think someone else has found it. But my really good ones, they never see the light of day. I've got some quite good quality ones that people have bought me as presents.

I really like guns. Again, it's a small, portable machine, very efficient. And probably if I had a lot of money I would have guns as a collection. But probably replicas – as a weapon to destroy or maim or kill, no. I've shot birds when I was younger, but I couldn't even do that now. I mean I just look at a bird, how small it is when it's dead, and you look at the thing you've done it with, which is like a thousand years of technology, and that's what you achieve, and it's pathetic. I used to quite enjoy shooting bottles and cans with an air rifle. And I'm interested in the ballistics of air rifles, I've read quite a few books on air rifles and that sort of thing.

War I am interested in war films and war books, yes. Which seems a bit of a contradiction considering that I'm anti-war, but I always wonder how I would react in the circumstances. Would I run, would I be brave, could I stand it, would I get shell-shock? *Saving Private Ryan*, that was an incredibly realistic film. How would I have made out? What does appeal to me is that I've been in situations which were not necessarily dangerous, but with guys that were undergoing a certain amount of hardship, and it often brings out the best in people. And I can see that in a lot of war situations guys not necessarily had a good time, but made the best of the situation they were in, and their better qualities came out. You need to put people in extremis, a lot of the time, to find out what they're like. And a war situation is the most extreme form of extremis you can get, I would imagine.

Also, I see the sort of cock-ups that were done in different campaigns, and I see the same sort of thing on a much smaller scale in the industry that I've been involved with. Instead of people getting killed, they're just expensive cock-ups a lot of the time.

Role models Maybe if my father had been there for my formative years I would have modelled myself on him, but there again it happens so often that as one matures, the hero one has looked up to turns out to have feet of clay, and disillusionment is a hard pill to swallow.

As I've said, I didn't want to be like my stepfather under any circumstances. As for substitute fathers, the only guy I might have wished had been my dad was my mother's best friend's brother, May's brother, Peter. He was in the army, I think he was in the Artillery, in the Middle East. I was very young then, perhaps six or seven, or younger, and he was in uniform, and was treated like a hero, especially when he came home wounded. It was discovered that he'd dropped some shells on his foot, that was the extent of the wound, but nevertheless. He was big and outgoing. But I mean I don't remember that much.

Apart from him I can't think of any man at all that I've ever thought of as a role model. I have never felt the need for a mentor. Which might seem odd. Maybe I was too independent for my own good. If life has taught me anything I suppose it is that whatever comes along has to be faced and no one else can face it for me. Even in my worst times I was always aware that I had to handle whatever was coming at me. My family and close friends have always been there for me but perhaps because of this I never needed to burden them with whatever crisis was present. This is probably from my childhood when as far as I can remember I never had a confidant, although I was possessive and jealous with my childhood friends.

Irish   I do identify with minority groups, yes, but particularly the Irish. I've had a long experience of them and got to know them very well. I'm known and am accepted by many of the Irish that have been in Brighton or worked on the gas for x amount of years. My friend Padraig said the other day, There must be a bit of Irish in you.

I think it's because our society categorises and stereotypes them, and I see something below the stereotype and find it interesting. I found the Irish uncomplicated, great sense of humour, an awful lot of them intelligent, and most important of all, they have natural good manners. Which I don't find here, amongst my contemporaries, for the most part. And they're lyrical. And they've been downtrodden and I do have the English characteristic of supporting the underdog.

A bit out of the ordinary   I like women like Peggy, who's the grand-mother of Stefan's partner. People would describe her as a character. She does knitting, she's got a machine, she sells jumpers. On one creation she did for herself, she worked into the back, in large letters, SOD OLD AGE. That sums up Peggy. Any woman who does that at the age of eighty-four has got to be top of my tree. She became an officer's wife, when her husband was in the army, because he came up through the ranks. But she never fitted the officers' wife's role and if she knew her place she certainly didn't keep to it. And that's the sort of character that I like. Someone a bit out of the ordinary. Quite often I like tetchy people because I find they're OK, they're far more honest.

Like is a strong enough word, I think, yes. Oh all right, I do feel fond of her but as I've got older I've been far more careful about opening the floodgates of emotion towards people, because it can be very damaging and can cause an awful lot of upset.

Touchy subject   There have been infatuations with women in the past, yes. Yes, yes. When I've opened, made myself vulnerable, yes. It's rather a touchy subject.

I would be obsessed, but it definitely wasn't just a matter of lust. You can fancy all sorts of people – and people do this through-out their life – you see someone that you're physically attracted to, whether you're married or not doesn't matter, it doesn't stop the urge going through your brain. That happens, full stop, both for men and for women, I don't believe it's an exclusively male thing.

I remember one particular episode, it only lasted I suppose for a month thank God. Purely in my head. All the poetic sort of non-sense that you associate with that sort of infatuation. I did write long letters that were never sent, and burned. What did they say? That if life was different, I could have chosen a different path, we could have made a go of it even though we were from two ends of the social spectrum.

Quite a lot of guys from my sort of background are fascinated by shall we say the Roedean accent. Because, well for a start you've believed from early on in life that intelligent middle-class girls are much better in bed than the other ones. I think that's a fallacy, it ties in with the myth of the convent-educated girl, that once they're loosened from all those restraints, they're wild, they blossom.

It was an adolescent feeling, yes. You'd get excited at a glimpse of the person, or if you heard their voice it would start a sort of reaction in you, a chemical reaction almost.

The fantasies were unworldly, nothing carnal. Possibly because the physical side of my life has always been very good anyway, so I didn't need that. I wasn't seeking something I wasn't getting anyway. Which made it in my head, on a higher plane. Idealised, yes, absolutely.

But I did find that everything became as though viewed through rose-tinted glasses, when I was in that state. People that really got on my nerves were bearable, and even pleasant, the days were shorter, and everything was like a form of drug-induced state. Ridiculous really.

New men & fried breakfasts   As I've said, I've never had a mentor and I always sort of found my own route or way of doing things, but on the other hand I still felt insecure and I didn't perceive myself as being attractive, no. No, just the opposite.

It's funny because at my age now I know that if I'd got the same sort of head on me when I was in my twenties, I wouldn't have had that fear of rejection, because I know there are ways of chatting up women and being acceptable without having pearly-white perfect teeth and a pimpleless skin.

I had that eye thing up till I was thirteen or so anyway, and even after thirteen people did notice the eye. And wearing glasses. I never thought I had the personality that went with wearing glasses. That sounds ridiculous, but I always assumed – when I was young, I don't think it now – that people with glasses were, not exactly bookworms or swats, but something like that, whereas I tended to get into all sorts of scrapes, physical and confrontational, and to forget – well not to forget, just to ignore – the fact that I wore glasses. They didn't fit the image, no. I even got into fights and didn't remove them, until they were smashed, when I was quite young.

But as far as women were concerned, I didn't do much about counteracting that. Other than being reasonably clean and using the right sort of aftershave. But I wouldn't prostitute myself as regards chatting up women as so many guys do. Being in love didn't make me particularly fluent, no, I had an awful line of chat. I couldn't give out the New Man bullshit that I used to hear guys giving to girls, and still hear. I know that an awful lot of guys use that sort of chat just to get inside a girl's knickers, when they're as chauvinistic as I am. And I do regard myself as chauvinistic. It's the classic story, where the guy is very attentive to his girl-friend, and the first day of the marriage he's sitting there with his sweaty vest and his braces demanding his fried breakfast.

Vulnerable   I never found it easy – and I think a lot of guys don't – to say, I love you, because you're making a commitment, and once you've made that commitment you're leaving yourself wide open, you've taken off the hard shell and you're vulnerable and you get very, very hurt. Have you ever seen a hermit crab out of its shell? It scuttles about in a panic because its great soft abdomen is exposed. I suppose I've had half a dozen rejections, that I can remember. I mean I don't think men have learned how to handle rejection yet, for all the New Man business. I know for sure that I found it awful, awful.

And because of the way that one tried to guard against it, you made yourself more likely for rejection. You know, trying to be more macho, and couldn't care less, and all that sort of nonsense. In fact, what it boils down to, you'd be trying too hard. You were more likely to be rejected, instead of trying to be honest and sincere.

Keeping up appearances   If I could afford to – I'm a bit of an extremist – I would dress extremely smartly. I won't compromise. I mean if I can't buy a suit from Armani for four hundred quid, I'm not going to buy it from the Co-op. I would dress smartly, because I know I'm the right shape and height to dress well. If I could afford to.

But that would be I think, to a degree, for Wendy's benefit. Because she is always extremely well turned out. For what income she has and what she does with it, I never fail to be amazed. She does it extremely well, she has very good taste. And she used to make her own clothes, quite a lot of the time.

I remember one incident when I had a suit, it was the suit I got married in. I bought it from Bernard Luper down Trafalgar Street, who was the Jewish tailor there, he used to actually go out into the street and try and drag you into his shop. But the suit started to wear out before I'd finished paying for the bloody thing. And we were walking somewhere or other and Wendy said, Do you know, in that suit you look like an old married man. The very next day I wore that bloody suit for work.

New baby   The birth of our grandson Jake has brought a lot of the past sharply into focus.

20. Peter holding his grandson Jake, summer 2000.

I've found that one of the ways of keeping him still is to sit him on my left thigh, and bring the other leg across but keeping the knee raised. All of a sudden, just getting in that position, there was this peculiar déjà-vu feeling, it just hit something in my memory, one of the few memories I have of my real father, sitting me down like this when I was very small. I remember clearly him telling me we were pretending this was the cockpit of a Spitfire and I was a fighter pilot. I hadn't thought of it for years, it just triggered that memory off.

Jake also reminds me of how little pleasure I had from my own sons when they were babies. I loved them, yes, but I didn't derive as much honest joy as I do from the latest arrival. The times were different and circumstances also. Now, maybe because I'm mature and less self-conscious, I can really let myself go and be as visibly affectionate and perhaps silly as I would like to have been those many years ago. To say I am overjoyed to be given this second chance is not overstating the case.

Part Three:

As Others See Us

FRIENDS

Dan

Rearing up If me and Peter had been in the trenches in the First World War, we'd have both been killed. Peter would have most likely got shot doing his duty and I would have been shot by a firing squad while trying to get away from doing my duty.

He'd be like putting his head above the parapet, and shouting and rearing up and getting it shot at, and then making us all suffer because they're shooting at us. My mate used to say, when Peter had a rear-up with the agent or whatever, Oh Jesus, we'll have to work hard this week, Peter's had a go at him, now he'll be putting the whip on us because he'll be frightened they'll be getting back at him, so.

Well it might mean we didn't get messed around, but there again it was a come-back on him in a certain way, that we'd have to work twice as hard, because now he'd stuck his neck out he couldn't back down, once we'd made a stand.

Peter took it all more seriously, to me it was just like a game, really. Sometimes I'd work, then I'd jack in and I'd go down the road or I'd shove off to America for a few weeks. But it's fair exchange, I mean I do my job, I don't mind working hard. But if I'd had enough I'd just walk away from it, it's not a problem. It doesn't mean that much to me, it's no kind of hardship to me. I mean sometimes it's like you're making problems for yourselves.

Old gangerman Peter says he caught me a couple of times leaving out things like a hammer or something, and he'd say, Right, are all the tools away? And I'd say, Yeah yeah. And he'd say, Well, what about the club hammer up beside the trench there? Then after that, every night when he asked if we'd put the tools away, I'd say, Yeah, we've put everything away except for whatever it is you're hiding behind your back.

Sometimes I see Peter like the old gangermen. I mean really he used to be a bit of a disciplinarian in some ways. In other ways he used to be kind of anti-social and didn't give a monkeys. One

21. Dan, portrait by Peter, 1987.

minute he'd want to be a revolutionary and the next minute he's saying, Where's the poxy hammer? I saw it as a game, I used to think, If it keeps him happy I'm not worried. As long as people aren't obnoxious and they're not threatening me, I'm quite easy to go along with.

As a ganger, he was good. He knew his job very well, and he did take a lot of interest. And just as well he did really, because we never. We was all mates but I suppose we were a bit younger, so he was like a bigger figure than us, kind of thing. And he used to rear up at us, he used to get us to do things, and we used to kind of shape up for him, so actually we could make life look better for him as well. Because we could tear into it and maybe do things better and quicker than the other gangs.

When we first started, years ago, I suppose that was the last of the old ways of working. It was like at the latter end of something that was established. It's like working on the docks, these were old-established rules, and they were just fading out when we come into them. You used to have fifty men digging up the street and gangermen going up and down like a ramrod, to make sure they've all got their backs bent and they're whipping it out. That's all gone by the board now, that's like a bygone age. Now, you're a two-man team, you all have to dig.

Wild colonial boys　And really we was young and silly. I mean me and Peter was like our own worst enemies, we used to work with our shirts off in the middle of winter, throwing pipes up on our shoulders, all icy, and a lot of that was just being macho. I mean when we was working piecework, we was wild and young. I suppose we were like a couple of wild colonial boys, we'd got to earn our money, spend it, just get through the next week trying to borrow and cadge, making our baccy last us. We used to work hard.

A kind of freedom　Peter could have done other things. I think he was totally come into that kind of game out of rebellion, really, against his parents and everything else. That's why I say to him now, I mean he gets really mad, Well all you've done is just done another geezer like me out of a job. Here he was, making a big thing out of being a foreman of a navvy gang, but with his attitude and his way, he was totally different from the rest of the guys. We were just there because that's what we happened to fall into, he was there because he'd rebelled against his parents. In the army, he could have been an officer, but he chose to be with the lads.

OK, it's not a bad choice, and OK, he likes being outdoors. But he could have gone up the structure and become an agent or something, I mean he would outstrip most of the agents I ever worked for, with his mentality, his education, everything. And if he'd still had the same kind of outlook on life he could have made things better for the lads from higher up, instead of fighting for us in the trenches at a very low level. He would have been on the other side, but I think a lot of the breakthroughs in life have come from the other side anyway. People that have got higher have got more clout, so they can actually do more, they can change things for a lot more people.

But I don't think he did want to be on the other side, he liked it with the lads. And he liked the crack as well. And the spirit, that's the thing about our job as well, I suppose, we could be a bit outlandish or say something a bit crazy, say pretty well what you want to say. As long as I'm not physically hitting somebody or being really disruptive, they'll say, Well let 'em carry on, they're still making us money, why bother 'em? You're not going to get another guy to come and do this work anyway. It gives you that certain kind of freedom.

Fights   The fight in the Seven Stars was a bit of a laugh as much as anything. We've had many a laugh like that. We've had some fights, really, me and Peter, in a certain way. We haven't been really violent, I don't think we're violent people. There was another Irishman we used to knock about with, now he was really violent. He was a boxer, but he never used his hands, he'd use a chair or anything.

But Peter can go to town. I mean he likes going to town, I think sometimes he don't mind me starting something because he likes the excuse to get going. I think he was having to prove things more than I have to. I will make it more of a joke. I think Peter's made himself hard, the way he was brought up and that. He had to make himself a lot harder than he was.

We got into a big fight years ago. I think that was on my eighteenth birthday, in a coffee bar. There was women hitting us with handbags and everything, in the end me and Peter had to fight our way out of that place. He whipped his glasses off there. He used to whip his glasses off quick and he used to like using his head a lot.

I think the fights started with drink, that was the big thing. When we was young, after the pub finished, you'd go to these coffee bars, and they stay open till one or two in the morning.

Best mate　Me and Peter, we've never really been one of the lads because, although we mucked about and had the crack, we've always been grown-up in our attitudes kind of thing as well. More of a grown-up outlook on life. I think he'd a very adult childhood in a certain way, and I did as well.

As far as I'm concerned he's my best mate, I've known him for years, I mean I know he'd do anything for me and I would virtually most likely do the same for him. Maybe we wouldn't say that to each other.

I think that's what we like with each other. I mean I just like him, but I don't really need him, and he doesn't really need me. I think that is the niceness about it, in a certain way. We're not dependent on each other. But if the chips were down he wouldn't have to say, we'd half know, I mean if he couldn't handle it, I'd dive in.

Seeing and looking　I knew he'd only got the one eye, but I didn't realise until later how poor it was. He was telling me that when we used to be working on night jobs, with gas masks on, he'd be virtually doing things by braille down the bottom of the trench. This was from really early on. So when you hear all this it gives you an understanding of why he used to have to be a lot more on the ball. By his intelligence, and by working things out, and even by taking a greater interest where maybe he wouldn't do if he had both his eyes. If we was doing a job tomorrow he'd be taking more interest in it tonight, where I'd just go tomorrow and start sorting it out. He'd be compensating. But there again, sometimes his actual eyesight is better because he's looking harder. I can see, but I don't really look a lot of the time. But when we were out fishing he'd see the dans long before I would.

So we knew, it didn't really matter. When he was waiting for his cataract operation we all kind of covered for him, so he could keep on working. We were working in a small gang, I suppose it could be like the army really, you can virtually all do each other's work. Obviously Pete used to have the shout, so he'd kind of say, Have we done it all?

But he's not like a lot of people with one eye, the way they look at things. When you see his head movements you wouldn't think he's got one eye, there isn't anything about him tells you he hasn't got two eyes. He must have a conscious thing about that, that he's learned himself to do.

Arguing   I've always got along well with Peter. We gee each other up, I think we kind of bounce off each other a bit. He tries to make me better myself. But we see things differently, we have arguments. I don't mind admitting I just talk out the top of my head, I just play it by ear as it comes along. Peter gets into a format, he comes well armed all the time. I can contradict myself, and he'll be picking it all up and I'll be trying to get out of it and it'll just kind of go on and on and on and on.

It's a kind of a game. He'll be on about his being a socialist and I'll gee him up, I say, Well, I'm a capitalist, and all the rest of it. We do sometimes come to some quite good conclusions by keeping picking at each other, you can actually unravel something and it makes you think, Oh I never saw it like that.

Sometimes, like when he's on about the holocaust and that, he'll see something in a book and he'll come rushing in, Have you heard this? And I say, Well so what? I mean I'm not shocked, Peter seems to be kind of shocked at certain things, and sometimes I think, Well why are you so shocked by it, I mean that's human nature, that's how things are. That's why I think he is quite soft, I mean he does feel for a lot of people.

Like now, he may be becoming an advocate. He'd be the perfect choice for the job. But sometimes he seems to be better at sorting my affairs out, maybe sometimes other people's affairs out, than maybe sorting out his own. I suppose if you're speaking on behalf of somebody maybe it's a lot easier than if you're doing it for yourself.

Perfectionist   He used to take things too seriously. Years ago, people he knocked about with, not me, used to call him Uptight Pete. He used to get uptight about a lot of things. And then when he gets uptight he can get nasty as well. A lot of his nastiness is out of fear or out of a reaction. If you get frightened sometimes, I mean I do, if I get frightened, I rant and act in a violent way. I think he'd be on the defensive thing a lot of the time. In general he's very competitive. You think, What are you competing for?

Put it this way, I find it very easy to work with him, but he finds it very hard to work for me. I think he has to be in control of a situation. I can work with people, I think, Well OK that's wrong, but if that's the way you want it done, so be it, as long as it's not going to hurt me. But Peter would say, Oh no, I'm not having it like that, or, Fuck you, and he'd be up the road. And really it wouldn't matter, because there's hundreds of different ways of doing things. He's a perfectionist, he wants it to be done his way.

Sometimes we argue, and he can come out with all the right reasons and everything else, but I still think he's wrong. I can't really say why, but I still think, That don't add up, to me. He's a really good debater, I mean he could talk to you black is white, but sometimes I know he's wrong and I can't put my finger on it, and I think, Oh well, so what. But if you leave it like that, he will fester. He's been awake all night once figuring something out, then he rings up the next day.

Professor Thirty years ago people thought I was just a thick prat, but now I'm classed as dyslexic. Peter reckons how I've lived life is through animal cunning. I know what he's saying, but I think quite a lot in front. I think what age I am now, I think where I'd like to be when I'm sixty. I mean when I get to a certain age, I want to have a certain control, I want to have a certain amount of finance. Maybe I can leave it to my children, or my grand–children, or as I said to Peter, I'd like to go on that Trans-Siberian Railway journey when I retire. Well I don't think Peter actually thinks like that. He's not interested.

The money we were making was never enough to keep us, that's just bread and butter. And with my situation, through being dyslexic and that, I realised I'd need a hell of a lot of qualifications to earn serious money. But I don't need any qualifications to go out and make my own money, save up and buy a house, or manoeuvres or certain moves. You just need to think.

Peter often reminds me of an absent-minded professor. He'll know how to do the job, he'll get wrapped up in gadgets and bits and pieces, but when it comes to making a cup of coffee, or taking care of business, he doesn't really want to know. In a certain way, he's got traits of the landed gentry, It's not done actually, we don't talk about money.

Suffering fools   I think in a certain way I've always landed right and Peter's always seemed to have confrontations. If he's living in a flat somewhere he'll have a bad landlord. Peter's in my car, I'm driving quietly down the road, and he's saying, Look at that fucking geezer! Have you see that? No I haven't seen that, man. I mean I haven't even noticed it.

He doesn't suffer fools very gladly, I've got a bone of contention with him because you know, we have this *Sun*-reading thing. He's on against it, he seems to be very damning on his own class. And I said to him, Well *Sun*-readers are a product of society, they've made people *Sun*-readers, it's not their fault.

He's very intelligent. I only have to say a sentence, and he can put his finger onto the button, he seems to have a sixth sense. I make a lot of sly remarks, and if you're being a bit lippy and you half say a word, he'll know what you're going to say next. Like yesterday he was on about his cats, he says one cat watches the television, and one cat doesn't, so one is more intelligent than the other. I said, Oh you've got a *Sun*-reader in the house as well then! He says, Don't you start!

But I've never really tried to analyse it, I've known him for so long, I think we just accept each other, to a certain degree.

Tony B

A sort of group   I met Peter in 1966. Some other friends and I decided to move to Brighton when we left Croydon Art School, and the guy who'd been head of Fine Art lived in Brighton. His name was Clifford Frith, grandson of Somebody-else Frith who was a famous painter. Peter was then living in New Steine. Clifford lived round the corner and Peter had got to know him, and I went down and got introduced to Peter.

We all used to go up to the local pub, the Royal Oak, on St James Street. We used to play bar billiards or darts. After the pub we'd go to Pete and Wendy's for their endless hospitality. It was handy after the pub. When you're young you don't so much think about going home, you want to carry on partying, whatever you do. People tended to go to Peter and Wendy's because it was hospitable and interesting and it was in the middle of Brighton. I met my first wife, Antonia, through Peter and Wendy.

It was a sort of group, mainly manual workers of various kinds, and other people who were arty. Antonia was middle-class, her father was a psychologist for the World Health Organisation, Peter always referred to her as Lady Muck. I was more of a factory worker, I worked in the silkscreen printing business at the time. There was Ann Clark, a local woman who I got to know well, we later shared a flat in Norfolk Terrace. She had a lodger, a fashion designer called Warwick Stone who now lives in California and does stuff for the Hard Rock Café chain. And there was Keith who lived upstairs from Peter and Wendy and later moved in with a woman called Deedee, two streets from New Steine. And Pete's friend Danny would come there sometimes, although he lived some distance away. And a couple of shipwrights, they were friends of Keith's. They worked over at Shoreham, in one of the big boatyards. Much later on, they were working on renovating a big Bristol Channel pilot cutter, right next to where Peter was sorting out his first boat. But they had no navigation skills so they ran it aground on its first voyage.

Conversation   So there was a mixture of people who were into ... I guess it was good conversation really. That was the common

22. Tony B at home, portrait by Peter.

denominator. The first time I met Peter he was easy to talk to and it carried on from there. I liked to talk, he liked to talk, and I guess that's how we got on. There's a lot of warmth there, although he was highly opinionated, with a sort of pretend gruff exterior. And gave no quarter in argument at all. But he doesn't ever fight his corner to try and win a point or put you down, he fights it because he knows he's right, or he's determined to get his point across, not at your expense necessarily. He's a very strong, determined person. Mind you, he will argue about anything, for the sake of it, but then so will I. He was interested in life, you know, learning things, finding out new things. Not settling into a pattern of any particular kind.

Loose and liberal   I suppose the group had somewhat left-leaning or liberal ideas, it was bohemian in being arty and loose and liberal and into drugs and whatever else it might be. But intellectual curiosity I think is the strong point, wanting to know things.

We were smoking dope, taking LSD and Speed – and going to work. Most of the time we all had jobs, none of us were layabouts. I don't think it was necessarily a strict work ethic, although the Protestant work ethic thing is certainly something I have, and I think Peter has. You probably just went to work because you needed the money and didn't particularly want to be supported by the state, it's that independence thing as well.

And there was work. You could have a job, give it up, and choose from another five, immediately. So I worked. Pete got me jobs, I worked on building sites, I found myself jobs in silkscreen printing places, it was very easy. You could pick and choose, you could go, Oh dear, don't like this job, I'll go and work in the bakery all night, Oh no, I don't like this, I'll stop that, and so on. There was a certain amount of freedom about it. Times of full employment.

Psychedelic strangeness   The pub was very much a laddish thing, I think, in those days. There were a couple of women, but Wendy would rarely go. At their flat in New Steine, after the pub, there could be anything from about four to eight people. The kids would be in bed. We'd hang around, and I suppose we were all younger, so it didn't actually matter about going to bed so much. It was kind, because Pete and Wendy would have to stay up and be hospitable till people went home. I suppose we got thrown out, or just wandered off, or they said, Right we're going to bed now.

I think as more drug-taking took over, and more acid, pubs didn't seem quite so interesting any more, so we went there less and less. This would be 1970-ish. We'd spend more time in each other's houses.

So there was a lot of psychedelic strangeness going on. I moved away, in '72. By then I was working in Unicorn Bookshop in Brighton, publishing books and things. Then we closed up in Brighton and moved to West Wales where we had a sort of communal farm and printing place. We had a printing press in the barn and we sat around the kitchen table binding the books, and we had cows and chickens and stuff like that, and vegetables. There were five of us to start with, then another couple of people came along, who were friends, to do more of the farming. I was driving round the country delivering books, so I'd go to Brighton every six weeks or something and I'd see Peter and Wendy. And they came up to the farm a couple of times, so we stayed pretty close friends.

Then I moved back to London in '75. Knockabout Press sort of grew out of the Unicorn Books in Wales. It was comic books like the Fabulous Furry Freak Brothers comic, and Fat Freddy's Cat, and books, marijuana growing guides, and more serious drug information books about cocaine use and abuse. It wasn't promoting drug culture, that existed already, it was more giving people correct information about drugs. Trying to let people understand the difference between different drugs, in the same way that the rest of us understand the difference between a pint of beer and a pint of whisky.

Almost family   Since moving to London we've gone down to Brighton to visit Pete and Wendy, or they've come up to see us, every couple of months.

Peter's a close friend certainly. I've always felt very fortunate that I've probably got maybe five or six friends I could turn up to in the middle of the night, bleeding or rain-soaked and in a state, and they'd just let me in and give me a cup of tea and it wouldn't be a problem. I wouldn't like to put one on top of the other.

I wonder if a lot of us are friends and almost family because we don't have any living parents or aren't close to the ones we have.

One of the things that Peter has in common with the other people that he's closest friends with, is a naughty sense of humour, in the sense of debunking things. Taking life very seriously and being very responsible for yourself and your family, and not doing damage to other people; taking social skills seriously, but not taking authority and established things seriously nearly so much.

Breadwinner   In the early days I don't think any of us felt we were treating women badly, they were certainly coming into their own, through feminism and whatever else. And men were still the breadwinners to an extent, there weren't nearly so many women working. When you go out early in the morning and come back exhausted, you don't run the house, you don't know where things are, you don't choose what colour's going to go on the walls,

you don't decide where the photographs are going to be kept. I
don't think it was any more laddish than this new laddish thing
that goes on now. There was quite a lot of respect for women, in
that rather patronising, old-fashioned way. But it was a laddish
thing when we were on our own, we'd be making rude comments
about women, telling jokes, or whatever.

It must be very difficult for Peter, having been the main breadwinner and supporter of the family for the past nearly forty years,
to be now not working, not providing money as before. But he does
produce the vegetables and makes stuff for the house and garden.
It isn't a question of not being able to fill his time. I'm sure he
could live three parallel lives and fill them all with activity. But a
bit of money helps. It would be nice to have enough money so that
if you see something about an event, an exhibition, a show or a
new consumer durable you can just do it or get it without having
to think about whether your bills will be paid at home. As far as
I'm aware no one in his family or friends thinks any less of him
since he had his heart problems or sees him belittled by not working. It's got to be better now than the shitty job it had become,
where any pride you took in your work was undermined by lack of
men, lack of equipment and bad organisation. It's not working in
the dirt that is the problem, it's being treated like it.

Alertness Because I love him so dearly I keep thinking of ways
in which I could help him to relax and take life a bit easier, but
then I realise I can't do that myself. I want Peter around for another ten years – he'll read this and go, What! Only ten!! – and
although I'm sure the heart surgery is great, once it's weakened
you, you need to take care. Pete's thought about this stuff, in fact
he's written a poem about it, but it doesn't do to dwell on it. I
wish it had never happened, but now maybe it gives a chance to
live an easier and less stressful life – if it wasn't for the bureau-
crats, the landowners, the politicians, the arms dealers, multi-
national polluters, royalty, next-door neighbours, family and friends
and that bloke on the telly, to name but a few.

I think in some ways Pete liked his stress. He has forced himself
to be who he is. It's this thing of always being ready for the unex-
pected, ready for a fight. Not that he's had lots of fights in his life,
but just in case somebody wants a fight you have to be ready. You
have to be ready for the argument, you mustn't let your guard

down at any time, otherwise somebody might do something unimaginable to you. I don't think it springs from fear, but it's some kind of alertness, not wanting to have one put over on you. Intellectually believing that people are downtrodden and also to an extent feeling you are downtrodden in life. He's ready for things to go wrong, he's got his hand out ready to catch the next disaster.

When he comes to my sister's house, and he's known her for a long time, he'll be like a new boy at school, terrified he'll do something wrong, very stiff in the way he behaves. People don't actually care whether you sit with your legs crossed or uncrossed. They don't want you to be wound up and over-polite.

And yet he never seems tense in conversation if it's one to one or he's sitting round at home or at our place.

Peter has perhaps that odd thing of being both a kind, pleasant person who doesn't go out of their way to start arguments, but will instantly snap into irritability or aggressive argument because of something someone says. I empathise with that position. I'd be a saint if it wasn't for other people. Perhaps he needs to see a stress counsellor to learn some tricks about relaxing. I don't know if it changes you but it may help in coming to terms with yourself.

No side   There is a traditional male thing that Peter has, to protect and control your family at the same time. It is his consistency that has made his children feel so secure, not forgetting Wendy's part as super-mum. Perhaps that's why they have lived at home for such a long time. Peter is so interested in people and so interested in children and young people. His kids' friends from down the years have become his friends, so that they feel quite happy about visiting with him and Wendy on their own, which is pretty unusual. He talks to them as if they are human beings, while still letting them know who is boss. There is no side to Peter, what you see is what you get, in the modern jargon.

Raising the tone   Pete remembers his childhood with crystal clarity. Or when they came by train to Carmarthen, he would know the number of the engine he was on. He's got this fastidious memory.

I can't think of specific highlights, in that way. I remember the tone of it more. I always looked forward to seeing Pete and Wendy, still do. It raises the tone of life, to an extent.

WENDY'S STORY

Life before Peter   I was born in Brighton. My family lived in Ewhurst Road which runs between Coombe Road and Bear Road. I grew up there and lived there right up until the time I got married, so I'd never had any experience of being on my own. My mother died when she was only fifty-four. I was eighteen and I started going out with Peter in November '58, which was only two months after she died. When I first left school I'd started on the haberdashery department in Vokins for a couple of years, then I worked in three offices and ended up working for a couple that had a greengrocer's in East Street, Mr and Mrs Nash. Then I moved to Benson's, another shop in East Street, which was a bit like a village.

Parties   The people I was knocking about with were just a crowd that liked traditional jazz, I think there was more of that than anything else. We used to spend most of our time in coffee bars and going to parties, didn't do a lot of drinking.

I don't know how to describe myself really. I was always rather shy. It might not have been always obvious because I felt embarrassed about being shy and I tried to cover it up. According to Pete I was trying to be sophisticated.

I never went to the Regent Ballroom. That was still quite popular in those days, but I never learned ballroom dancing. We only danced at parties, bopping, just doing kind of free dancing, that's what we did. A bit of necking, sitting around. Those were the highlights of one's life, at the time. I liked Elvis Presley, we were getting into rock-and-roll then. I even used to dance on my own at home to my records, I had a little dansette record player. I remember dancing my feet off one day, and I actually made them bleed. Carpets aren't very good with bare feet, if you're doing a lot of spinning about.

There were several of us who went to art school, so we liked to think we were on the fringe of that sort of thing. And we knew a few French boys that came over and were studying here. Still got a picture of one, I don't know why I remember him so well, I only

went out with him very briefly. But he was quite dishy. We used
to go to jazz clubs and Tingey's coffee bar and the Espresso in
North Street, which was where I met Peter.

Something clicked   We were a bit bohemian in the way we dressed
I suppose, whereas Peter was more or less verging on a Teddy boy.
He tended to be hanging around up the Espresso coffee bar and
we just got chatting one day. It wasn't love at first sight exactly,
not just by looking at him, no. Before I actually knew him I remember thinking he was always blinking a lot. And he'd got a
very small nose. I don't know why, they sort of struck me. But
then as soon as I got to know him, even very early on before I'd
spoken to him, there was this change. Those things weren't there,
I just didn't notice them any more.

I know he got very paranoid about his eye. He didn't tell me
straightaway about only having one eye. I can't really remember
how soon he told me, but it wasn't that long into the relationship because he'd lost one girlfriend when he told her. As though
he'd become very wary, thinking, If I tell her this, is she going to
throw me over? But then on the other hand he actually wanted
to tell me, to get that bit over with, I suppose. But to me it was
immaterial, I didn't think that made any difference to him. I suppose you could see there was something different about the eye
but it didn't occur to me at first that it was artificial. You don't
notice it much.

I just sort of clicked. I can't pinpoint any real reason. He's a
very good talker, oh yes, but I don't remember that as being the
reason. Also from the time we met to the time when he asked
me to marry him was only just over a week, so we didn't have
time to do that much talking, at all. It must have been physical, I
suppose. Or maybe he's got whatever it is Stewart's got that seems
to draw women from miles around even when he treats them,
you know, not perhaps as considerate as he might. I've known
a few women over the years that seemed to think he was quite
attractive.

I think he and Brian gave me a lift home one night from the
coffee bar, and so the next time I went up there they started chatting and they were having a party at Brian's place and they
invited me, and I was always up for a party. So I went along and
ended up staying the night and having to tell a load of fibs to my

father, and I don't know, something clicked, and after that it was not much over a week according to my diary that he asked me to marry him.

Marriage guidance   When I look back now it just seems ludicrous that I could have possibly thought I knew what I wanted, that quick. But it seems I did. Not that long after we'd met I had this feeling that my mother somehow got into my mind and told me it was all right and that I should go ahead with it. I remember feeling quite strongly that she approved, that it was OK and he was the right one. There's been many times over the years when I've had qualms and second thoughts along the line and I've said, Bloody woman, you were wrong, mother! But as it's turned out I think she was right.

Passionate   The first sexual relationships I ever had, I didn't know what I was doing. It seemed to be an extension of when you'd been to the movies and seen them kissing, I presumed that was part of it. But I didn't know that was what you did to have babies. I just didn't know.

Pete and I did sort of jump into bed straightaway, yes, the night of the party, about the second or third meeting. I think it was my frilly petticoat and my dark stockings that did it. My dad was working nights, so Pete used to stay the night and go off in the morning, very often before my father came home from work at seven o'clock. It was all very passionate and I suppose that lasted for the first six years.

We did know about contraception, yes, but I don't know that they did give them out then, if you were under age. We kept our fingers crossed. Pete said it should have been legs crossed. I think pregnancy was just the next state, because it was still very much thought that that's what you did, that's what girls did. The attitude was that when you were grown up the next thing was getting married and having babies.

I can't really remember the incident that led up to the fight in the coffee bar. I expect the guy made some sarky remark. For the whole of the next fortnight, until he actually saw the guy again and went to have the fight, he was so difficult you couldn't talk to him. So I felt the best thing was to let him have a bit of a go and then things would get back to normal. Which is why I did hold someone back from trying to stop the fight. He was a weight-lifter but he was not very big.

Wedding   When we'd been going out for a bit over a year we got married. We had the wedding reception at home. We came back from the Registry Office, it was February and it was hailing and snowing. And we had a wedding cake I'd bought, and everything else I'd been rushing around preparing in the morning. And after the reception, which was by mid-afternoon, we had to move into the flat that we'd got in Clifton Terrace. The landlady and land-lord there were the greengrocers I'd been working for, Mr and Mrs Nash.

For our honeymoon we went to London Zoo. At least we got some blurred black and white – well grey and white – pictures taken from the train on the way up, and some of the Zoo.

It was quite a nice flat, we had the garden over the road from there that you could use. And we got on well with Mr and Mrs Nash. When Mark was born she was very good when I first came home with him, she helped me bathing him and things like this, because I knew nothing and it's quite a daunting prospect, you've got this tiny wee thing that you know nothing about.

The time in Spain was something I'd never experienced before. I'd not been abroad, so that was something very different and fas-cinating to see. Going up into that village, the reaction we got from people there was really so you felt like some sort of celebrity.

Hard times   Then Whippingham Street was a bit of a disaster all round really. I can remember being upset a lot of the time, hear-ing her steps coming down and then the door bell going and dread-ing answering it and, oh dear, feeling in constant turmoil from day to day, thinking maybe this was going to be another day she was going to tell us we had to leave, until she changed her mind a few hours later. And the fact that I was pregnant probably didn't help matters, because you tend to be even more emotional, I mean it was a strain anyway.

I got toxaemia and had to go into hospital. Although that's a physical thing I think all those pressures we'd had throughout my pregnancy did have an effect on my physical being. We decided we couldn't live there, we'd have to get out, and we found this top flat in Devonshire Place. So there was all the strain of the previous place, and moving house. My sister's husband Clive helped us move because Pete had to work and I didn't feel I could leave Clive to lug everything up the stairs, so although I was seven months pregnant with Stewart I felt I had to do my bit of lugging.

And then it was only a month after the move that the ceiling fell down, and we had months of mess on top of everything. We were living on top of each other with all the furniture from the room where the ceiling had fallen down stacked up in the bedroom and at the eating end of the kitchen, which was a long narrow room. So that you couldn't use the kitchen properly and we had to sit on the bed in the bedroom to eat. I had to try and dry the washing in the kitchen, and one thing and another.

Needs must We had to carry everything up the stairs and if I ever forgot the odd thing it was a duck-billed nuisance because I'd then got to go back again. The push-chair came apart into two sections, so you'd take one bit down, then go up and take the other bit down, then go up and get the baby and take the baby down, and then anything else. And when you came home you'd just got everything up there and then you went, Damn, I've forgotten the, whatever. It was on the third floor, but you had several half landings. A lot of steps.

We had one of those shallow old earthenware-type sinks, and the water used to leak from behind it. The electric meter was right under the sink. I had to wear rubber gloves when I put the shilling in the slot, because the thing was live. When you emptied the shillings out, there was all rust on them because there was that amount of water inside the meter. So Peter got a stainless steel sink off a site. And when we had the plumber guy to fix the sink, we'd warned him that sometimes the meter came live. He was using a blowtorch under there to melt that stuff, soldering or whatever, smoothing all that out where the U-trap was, and he touched it and it threw him into the bedroom, and his blowtorch caught the flax and stuff alight, but he managed to get himself together and put it all out quick.

Anyway they fixed the stainless steel sink in but then I went to do the washing-up one night, and I'd got rubber gloves on, but as I touched the side of the thing with my wrist, I felt an electric shock. I said, It's definitely live. I had to put Peter's wellies on as well, so I was in my nightdress and wellies and pink rubber gloves.

201

There was one bathroom and toilet in that place, which we had to share with the rest of the house. You'd got a family of two adults and two children on the ground floor, you had sometimes one, sometimes two people in the front room, then you had three people on the floor below us, then us. So if you had two people go in and have baths on the trot, you ended up having to go up Rock Gardens to go to the toilet. It wasn't a good place to be, it's not surprising there were a lot of pressures. There were so many things that made life difficult. When you look back on it, it seems even worse, you think, How did I put up with it? But we had no choice.

Rows   I think the rows and walk-outs we had there were down to the crowded circumstances of living. One of the times, we'd been arguing on the Saturday, quite a lot of row, and it started up again on the Sunday morning, and that really upset me. I was going to leave. But when I got to the bottom of the stairs there was a wash-boiler that my dad had brought over for me and I thought, Oh, I suppose I'd better go and do the nappies first. I dragged this wash-boiler up all these flights of stairs, I wouldn't ask Peter, and did my washing and the nappies. By then things had improved a bit. So I decided I wouldn't leave after all.

Tail comb   Then we had to move to a one-room flat on the first floor and the house was sold. Marie, the new landlady, lived underneath. And the children would just run up and down and she'd bang on the ceiling, and it would be very wearing trying to keep them quiet enough, trying to keep kids virtually stationary. She hadn't got children and didn't appreciate that sometimes they are going to run up and down. They've got a lot of energy and you can't be taking them out all the time, there are other things you've got to do. Even in one room and a kitchen you've still got a certain amount of cleaning, and I had all their washing and one thing and another to sort out, which was difficult in a small flat.

And one of the times, when she'd been knocking on the floor, Mark ran across the room again. He must have been five. I was out the kitchen, and, oh dear, I just thought, God we're going to end up losing this flat, and I suppose everything was getting to me, and I was in the middle of doing my hair. And he ran across the room and I stuck my head round the door, threw the comb across the room and shouted, shouted, Just stop, and shut up, stop keep running up and down! And the comb flew across the room and caught him between the eyes.

It was a metal tail comb, so you have that pointed end to it. And of course blood gushed out of his head and I said, Oh my God, what have I done now, I'll have to take them, I'll have to take him to the hospital, and I'd got a nappy there which I was mopping the blood up with, and I had to get Stewart ready to take him as well, and Stewart was I don't know how old, he wasn't walking at that stage, he was quite a small baby. And so I couldn't pick Mark up, to carry him up the road, because I had to carry Stewart, and I got up to Edward Street, tried to flag a car down, and ended up walking some distance towards the Royal Sussex trying to stop a car to see if somebody would give me a lift with a baby in my arms and Mark beside me holding this thing up at his face. And eventually an elderly couple stopped and took me along to the hospital, and they stitched him up.

Build-up   And I got really sort of frantic, I was thinking, Oh my God if they find out what I've done, you know, they'll think I'm awful. I didn't really feel that I'd deliberately set out to do him damage, but it could have been an eye, and not just his head. And I didn't tell Peter. He didn't find out for years.

When he'd had his stitches in I came back from the hospital and as I came through the hall, past Marie's door, she came out, and she said, Oh what's happened to Mark? And I said, Oh he fell on my comb, which is what I'd been saying at the hospital, and I think I kept saying that this was what had happened because that's what I wanted Mark to say if anybody should ask him, because I didn't want anybody to know that I was so awful, that I would hurt my little boy. And she was sort of, Oh you should have asked me, I would have looked after Stewart, I could have come up the hospital with you. But I didn't feel I could say, But it was because you'd been banging on the ceiling and he ran across the room that the whole thing had happened. I didn't say it, I never said that.

Things just got on top of me and it's all out of proportion to things that are going wrong at the time. I know that's what caused me to get more annoyed with things the kids would do. They can put quite a lot of pressure on you at times. And it would gradually build up and there'd be one thing they'd do which wasn't that bad, but that was the last thing, and that would make me lose it. I used to hit them, and smack them, yes. I did.

Then eventually I'd calm down. Whenever I'd had a bit of a rant and a rave with the kids, nobody could do anything enough for me afterwards, it would be all sweetness and light. And I would calm down and it would be all right. But then I'd feel very bad when they were asleep and you look at them and there they were looking like little angels and you'd think, Oh God, tomorrow I must try and not get so uptight about things.

Sometimes we'd fall out when we were trying to keep the children quiet. It used to work both ways. Sometimes he'd be the one that would have a go at them and I'd get annoyed about it, I'd say, They're just being children, they're not doing anything wrong. And he would do the same to me when I was the one that was jumping on them. Because you knew it wasn't really right.

But overall things did get better when we moved to New Steine.

Aggression   My father was not an aggressive man by any means, and then there was my sister, my mother, my aunts, and one of their husbands had died, so there was more women around than there were men. So there hadn't been much in the way of aggression in anybody I'd ever grown up with.

I don't know whether it would have seemed worse if it had been coming from somebody else, but for the most part, because I knew him as Peter, and quite intimately, somehow it didn't seem to frighten me as much as it might have done if it had been somebody else. I have been frightened of him when we've been having rows and fights, and we have had physical set-tos. He chucked me down some stairs once. He even knocked my teeth in. That's why I've got this damaged one in the middle.

Violence   I never did anything after any of the physical violence. I'd probably been shouting somewhat before. The time when he knocked my teeth in, what brought it on was that he and Alan, that was the husband of the couple that used to spend a lot of weekends with us at New Steine, had just popped up the road to have a 'quick drink' or a 'quick game of bar billiards', or whatever it was. They 'weren't going to be long'. And they were. Because Marina had been up there, this Russian girl we knew, and another one called Lynn, and a few other people, they'd ended up staying up there some while.

And I got annoyed about it. I didn't say anything when he came back, I had vowed to myself I wasn't going to react, I wasn't going to shout, I wasn't going to do these things, but he kept on at me, he wanted something. I said there was nothing wrong. Oh yes there is. No there isn't. Come on, tell me, I want to know what's wrong. And in the end I accused him, Oh it was because Marina and Lynn were there so I suppose that would be more interesting than being at home with me, these silly things that I would come out with when I was angry. Not because I seriously believed them, but because you feel you want to say something to hurt somebody when you're annoyed with them.

And of course I got all irate and was shouting and he grabbed hold of me and nutted me in the teeth. When I felt my mouth, my teeth were in, I shouted, Oh, you've knocked my teeth in. I went rushing into the bathroom, I pushed them back again. But one was cracked and has never really fully recovered and I've had quite a bit of treatment on it. I told the dentist I fell down the stairs. I expect he'd heard that before. But then if you did fall down the stairs and you went and said that to your dentist, he'd probably think you were lying anyway, so I don't suppose it matters a lot really.

Remorse   Over the years I found out that he did feel remorse afterwards when he saw me with my thick lips or whatever – I got a cut down here, just under my lower lip where the bottom teeth went through, that was the other time. I think sometimes I probably had stirred him up, I'm sure I was not without total blame.

Obviously I didn't enjoy it. On the other hand I never felt, Oh my goodness, I can't stay around if you're going to do this.

Anger   Afterwards he never ever felt like he could say sorry, because he said that if he did something he did it because he meant to do it, and so he wasn't going to be sorry afterwards. I mean when he gets angry he's far more calculating than I would be. When I get angry I just lose it, but he gets very clear-thinking. The few times I've seen him when he's been really angry about somebody, I mean it really is quite a frightening experience. His whole face just loses its colour and goes ashen and it gets drawn, like with the cheeks sucked in, and it's really frightening. I don't think he's ever got like that with me.

Jealousy   Oh there have been times I've been scared of Peter when he's been brooding about things and thinking things over, very often. He keeps things up for quite a while. He wouldn't just converse normally, because he'd be sitting there just thinking thinking thinking, and then eventually he'd start talking about whatever it was that was troubling him. I always felt a bit like I was being interrogated, because of his jealousy. And his mind is so different to mine. He'd be thinking, and reading things into things that had never even occurred to me. And it was all down to this jealousy. He'd sit and think and think and think.

I think some of the jealousy was, oh, insecurities on his part. He didn't always feel confident about himself, and there was always this chance I might find somebody else more attractive and become more interested in them. But it probably wouldn't have been like that, because I never feel I evaluate people by their attractiveness. I find people's attractiveness grows when you get to know them, if you like them, whatever the first impression is.

Feelings under wraps   He can still brood over something, but he'll probably talk about it with me more. He's never been much of a one for talking about his feelings, but I think all this stems from the fact that when he was growing up, being with foster-mothers, he had to keep so many feelings to himself. And being away at boarding school, you had to keep all your feelings under wraps. And you don't spend years keeping your feelings under wraps and then suddenly snap your fingers and bring them out in the open, it doesn't work like that. He was very bad at being demonstrative with his feelings for many years.

Although while I was in hospital after the birth of Mark he wrote little loving messages throughout the magazines he brought. I still have them somewhere.

Like a lot of men with their children, with the first one he was quite sort of awkward, and didn't do much in the way of helping, but I think it was probably because he didn't really know how to. I know he loved Mark. He didn't take the pram out and things like this much, but then men didn't really, then. New men weren't in view at that point. But he would push the pram sometimes if we were out together. Whereas with the subsequent ones he did, he was more involved, I mean not a great deal, but then he didn't really have a lot of time because he was always at work.

I think he found it very difficult when I was in hospital with toxaemia, the month before Stewart's birth. He and Mark stayed at Jean Bartlett's, who was an ex-landlady of Pete and Dan's before we were married. It was difficult and distressing for him, being at work from 7.30 am to 6 pm and visiting me in hospital. And for Mark, he wasn't three yet. Pete had to wake him when he got back from work to chat and play with him. On Sundays I had to look out of the hospital window, children were not allowed in the wards. Mark was very clingy on my return from hospital which was very understandable.

Chauvinism   He was a chauvinist. Like when he went fishing, he never knew quite what time he was coming back. It would be a bit vague, but even the vague time he could give never bore any relation to what time he actually came home. And when he did arrive, sometimes it was with Alan, sometimes it would be with Danny, or whoever. And no matter what I was doing, it was, How about a cup of coffee then? Or, Where's my dinner? And yet I'd been waiting around for hours, thinking he might be back around four, say, and he didn't get back till seven or eight. And I'd be expected to wait and it was always, Jump, as soon as he came in the door.

It wouldn't occur to him to make the coffee, oh no, no. You don't have a dog and bark yourself, was always his motto. The first time he ever made a drink was after we were married twenty-seven years. I don't think he knew where the things were kept. So I don't know whether I've got enough time left now to get him cooking the dinner.

He does sometimes do the potatoes and he did say the other day when he was doing the potatoes with us, It's a bloody good job I didn't learn to cook, I'd be insufferable, chefs are meant to be temperamental. I said, Yes that's a point, I do all the cooking round here, it's about time I got a bit more temperamental then isn't it? He said, No it's not the women, it's the men who get to be temperamental.

It's difficult to tell whether the arguments and difficulties we used to have throughout so much of our married life were just

23. Peter and Wendy in the kitchen at Worcester Villas, about 1980.

because Pete was as jealous and as chauvinistic as he was, or whether perhaps that would not have been such a problem if we'd had less pressure. I think the main problem is probably the lack of space and money. Pete worked hard all the time, he couldn't do any more than he did and I never ever felt it was his fault we were short of money. You can't get back at the person. It's society, just the way things are. But it does put a strain on you, you feel it's got to come out somewhere.

Turning point   Things were at a very precarious point at the time we moved to Worcester Villas in 1976, the prickliness and diffi-culties between us had built up to quite a crescendo. I think there was a period when I did even feel indifferent, yes. And that was the worst bit. I mean, to feel resentment and anger, even pangs of hate occasionally, at least you're getting feeling, but when you don't feel anything, that's bad.

But the move was a turning point. At first, with moving and a lot of other things taking up your time and thoughts, you don't have too much time to think about feelings and the relationship. And then more or less straight on top of that Pete went through the trauma of having the cataract operation and the possibility of losing his sight. This might have brought on a change of feeling, yes, because the night before he went into the hospital, we went out the garden together and he just wanted to look at the sky, and the stars, just in case tomorrow, he wasn't ever going to see them again, you know, and things like this. And I remember feel-ing quite emotional with him, at that time.

That was such a traumatic time, because if things hadn't gone right he would have been blind at the end of it and I knew that if that happened I wouldn't be able to go, I couldn't desert him. Whatever difficulties or resentments might have been around some of the time, in the earlier days, you don't spend that long living with somebody without having some foundation there. There were times I felt that perhaps feelings had gone totally out of the win-dow, but obviously they couldn't have done, because I still felt some-thing that kept me there.

Renewal   I suppose his attitude changed. I've always thought that he felt things had got to a very bad point and he did really make a conscious effort then to temper down some of his more extreme reactions and aggressive way of behaving towards me. He did. I felt that seemed to make it easier, he was nowhere near as brusque and chauvinistic.

After the move financial circumstances were easier and we were also able to be more relaxed because there was more room, and if you're feeling a bit prickly you can keep a bit of space between you, so a lot of the things that might have blown up into arguments, don't, they just blow over instead. And that's when I realised how much pressure living in such confined circumstances had made. We could just get to build up our relationship, rather than continually having goes at it, like we had been over the years. It was just having space to get away from each other when we needed to.

So we picked up all the ends again and built it up, and it felt like falling in love again, if you like, to me. It definitely felt as if we were starting things over again. In my mind it felt like that.

Paid work   I'd given up work when I got married, because I was about to have a baby. Then when the boys were little I used to go and do a bit of cleaning, because I could take the pram along with me.

At Worcester Villas we had students for a few years, to help with the rent, and for the most part enjoyed them. Then I got a bit fed up with always sharing the house with somebody else that you were unfamiliar with, nice as they were. I ended up getting the job at the chemist in Hove Villas, where I still am. I quite like just chatting to people. Although I'm shy, I don't feel shy at work, because you get familiar with the surroundings, it's not like being in a strange place where I would feel more awkward. And a chemist's is more interesting than your average shop job, there's quite a bit more involved with it. You learn that much more than you would just selling.

Home work   I've never felt in the least career-orientated. I find quite a sense of achievement in running a home, and that's one thing I will definitely say in Peter's favour, despite any jealousies and chauvinism or anything, he always seems to have appreciated what women do when it comes to bringing up a family. He appreciates that it's quite a job in itself, he's always maintained that over the years.

When the more radical feminists started coming on the scene and making a big thing about women having a choice, being able to do this, that and the other, I think they did rather put over the feeling that women that didn't want to go on and do something else were rather settling for the boring being tied to the kitchen sink routine. But I mean it's not really like that.

I suppose it depends very much on the person, some people wouldn't feel the need to do something else. Although circumstances pushed me into working, I've never felt compelled to be a career woman at all. And now I've obviously got enthusiastic with my gardening, and one thing and another. And I quite enjoy my painting and decorating, or when I can help design someone else's interior.

Ups and downs   When I look back over my life with Peter there have been many ups and downs.

During some of the downs I came very close to throwing in the towel and I certainly did get as far as thinking seriously about what might happen if I left him, because there were periods where I really wasn't very happy, about a lot of things. I don't say all the times were without justification, but I always felt that he started the ball rolling. But this all gets a bit personal.

We didn't separate, mainly because of the children, which were our shared responsibility, but also because I hadn't had any experience and I had my doubts about whether I could cope on my own. It does take the edge off the bad times if you have someone to share them with. I have no doubt that I would have had the children, providing I stayed single, because there's no way Pete would ever have had anybody else bringing up his children, because of his own experiences with his stepfather.

Maybe Peter didn't always see it as bleak or black as what I did at times, it's difficult to know. He's never really said. And I've always been a bit reluctant to go into it and really talk it over with him, because I think, Well you're more likely to stir up things you don't want to stir up.

All over again   Peter's strength of character, which can make him very single-minded, determined and stubborn, even to the point of seeming hard or definitely difficult, also works just as strongly on the loving, thoughtful, generous, protective and kindly side of his nature. He has always been able to make me laugh a lot. Many were the times he's had us all in stitches with the things he says and does.

In Worcester Villas there was a vast improvement in our accommodation with so much more space, the easing of finances, helped by taking in foreign language students and then my working part-time at the pharmacy, the boys growing up and becoming more independent, and the mortgage repayments becoming relatively lower. Our relationship fell back into place. For the first six years it had all been very passionate, then that just went below the surface for a while. And then came back up again, my love and respect for him blossomed, so I don't want to even think of life without him. With lovely sons we're proud of, what more could I want?

Would I do it all over again even if I knew of the hardships to come? I most certainly would.

MARK, STEWART & STEFAN: BREAKING THE CYCLE

Showing affection   As a father he was very passionate. He wasn't always loving. But when one looks back on it – you didn't necessarily think of it at the time – you feel it was always there, but he kept it hidden, he wouldn't have admitted it. It might be that he's got the loving feelings but he's not very good at showing them. Because of the sort of childhood he's had himself, he wouldn't have known how to show affection to a young child. And it's much easier to show anger than affection because anger's a shut-off point, whereas affection has got to carry on. But if you didn't care that much, you wouldn't get that angry either. It's two sides of the same coin.

He's not very domesticated, but he's not necessarily totally chauvinistic. He's probably a lot more thoughtful in a lot of ways, when it comes to other people having problems, than the rest of us.

At Christmas we'll get together at the end of the evening and wrap up Wendy's presents, and Peter will be writing the tags out for her. And he'll write really beautiful phrases and little notes and stuff like that to Wendy and he does show his affection to her, it's just that it's something he keeps to ourselves, as opposed to showing everybody.

Anger   Peter was a very feisty, angry, quick, hot-blooded sort of person when he was younger. Once his blood gets up, he's off. It's that self-protective thing. He used to be always very, not so much on edge, but ready to react. He is terrifying when he gets angry. His whole face changes, he goes grey and his cheeks go in. That was enough for most people. And that was the thing we also learned, growing up: when we saw that face you knew you move out the way, it doesn't matter whether you're right or wrong. But not so much now, as he's got older that's tempered down.

Once at New Steine we were playing about and we broke this bloody window and we were so scared that we went to bed at two o'clock in the afternoon, because when Peter come home, whatever time it was, if we were asleep he wouldn't touch us.

But it was the anger we were scared of, not so much of being hit.

Hit me too!   When Mark was about sixteen we'd arranged that we would go out night-fishing on the harbour-arm at Shoreham, just us three and a friend, Timmy. It was going to be an all-night session, we had a little pack lunch and stuff like that. Peter hadn't realised we planned to be out all night, but that didn't transpire till afterwards. So, the all-night idea was very nice, but when the time got to us, we were thinking, Oh we're not catching much, it's not that exciting, it's very boring, it's getting cold. So we decided to pack it in.

Then as we were coming home up the bottom part of Boundary Road, there's Pete walking down. This is about one-thirty in the morning, so there's not a lot of people around, it's a Wednesday night, something like that, it must have been during the winter holidays, it was cold and horrible, and we see this figure striding along the road with its hands deeply set in the pockets, and as it's approached, we sort of got as far as Hello, what are you here for? and it's like, Thump, Whack, Slap to Mark, and then Stewart said, If you're going to hit him you'll have to hit me as well. Which he did. Tim was just totally gobsmacked. Not literally of course.

Pete's version is that he was having visions of one of us being blown off the harbour-arm in the dark. He'd really started winding himself up and when he gets worried he also gets angry, it's part of the same deal.

King Kong   Or there was the King Kong episode. We never had a telly at New Steine because the landlord wouldn't let us have an aerial. So Stewart learned to lip-read at the Rediffusion shop down at St James Street. They had a touch-sensitive control on the outside of the window so you could change the channel. Excellent. One evening he was watching King Kong and Peter sent Mark down to get him, told him it was his bedtime, and Stewart said, Yes all right, I'll be back in a minute. And quite some time afterwards he was still there and Mark came down the second time. And then the third time it was Peter came down, and as he was standing watching Fay Wray it was a swipe to the side of the head, Boum, bedtime! So then he had to go home.

Good hidings   But he's always definitely been against any sort of ritual punishment. The smackings we got were because we'd done something that we shouldn't be doing, not just because we were being a bit of a nuisance, but because we were being right little effing arseholes. If you were being very specific or cold about it you could say we usually deserved it. It was done at the time of the offence so to speak, and invariably after warnings. And he wouldn't sort of continually remind you about it from day to day. It's the sort of thing we can laugh and joke about now.

The normal thing would be a slap, with a sweep of his arm. A cuff round the head. Just a couple of knocks, you wouldn't be like beaten around the place. And he would be under control. That's the difference between beating a child and punishing a child. Beating means when you've lost control and it's not because they've done something wrong, it's actually your emotions that are coming out and you're trying to hurt them. It was never that.

If we were given a good hiding, that would be a good whacking round the legs and that sort of thing, we were sat down and it was explained to us, Now you do know why you had that done to you, don't you? It wasn't just, give them a good hiding, and you think, Well what did I do?

White-hot   There was only once or twice that he really did wallop Stewart one that knocked him flying. Peter's version of it goes like this: 'a neighbour that lived in the street behind us at New Steine was constantly complaining about the kids. On this particular occasion something had gone wrong, I can't remember what, perhaps at work, or Wendy and I were having a row. Anyway this woman came to the front door. I don't know what she went on about but it was nothing very serious. I called Stewart into the room then asked this woman what she thought I ought to do to him. I didn't give her the chance to answer, but gave Stewart a serious backhander that knocked him across the room. I asked her, Was she now satisfied? She said nothing. I believe she was very shocked. Stewart didn't deserve this clout, but this bloody nuisance caught me when I was white-hot about something else.'

On the odd occasion that Peter did hit Stewart quite hard, he was really badly upset about it afterwards. You knew just by looking at him and that sort of thing that he was sorry. And yes, he would apologise, he did say sorry. He probably wouldn't say it there and then, but he might realise when he's had time to think about it.

Father advocate   Once three of us went to John Beal's in East Street, Stewart, Mark and our friend Gerry. And as we were leaving the store the assistant manager has collared us. Apparently some old pensioner had allegedly seen us shoplifting, so he'd come down along with the assistant to stop and search us. We certainly hadn't been doing anything to even look like we'd been shoplifting. So anyway we've gone home none the worse for wear, but then when Peter's got home from work and heard that his boys have had their pockets turned out for no apparent reason, he's grabbed us, grabbed Gerry as well, and stormed off to John Beal's just before they closed. And he's got the assistant manager and he's launched into him verbally, What reason did you have for doing that? And the man said, Oh, this lady ... And Peter said, Oh well, do you always do everything the public tell you to do? Look there's Jack the Ripper, go and do a citizen's arrest on him ... And creating a scene, which as we know people in this country don't like. And by the end of it this manager was like shrinking, backpedalling and on his heels, wanting to get out and disappear through the floor somewhere a bit quick, but obviously he couldn't, he had to put up with it, and he realised he'd made a mistake in what he'd done.

Hard on himself   He treats work as I think he treats everything, he puts his all into it. He's a perfectionist, oh Christ yes. I think that's to his own discomfort. He made it hard on himself. It rubs people up the wrong way. But then also if he didn't do that he probably wouldn't have the respect that he's got. I suppose we've always had the thing of being conscientious, the sort of work ethic.

Cool   When there has been a hazardous situation, he's one of these people who stays cool and can deal with it. There was that time up on top of the Dyke, when the digger driver ripped a stop-cock out of the top of this big high-pressure main. And this gas was just screaming out, it's going to take time for British Gas to get a crew up there to sort it out. So he's put on a full asbestos fire suit and then gone up and bashed a wooden peg into the hole, so as to prevent a lot of the gas coming out, because when

you've got a gas and air mixture which is obviously very dangerous, if you can restrict the gas flow with a wooden peg you don't
create any sparks. Anyway he did all that and was quite OK at
handling it.

Like father, like son   The two of us, Mark and Stewart, since the
merchant navy, have had a working life very similar to Peter's.
Stewart for example, because he started going out from six or seven
years old sort of thing, and picking up a shovel, already knew
how to do various bits of the work, through being with Peter. And
not so much liked it, but it was an easier option in a lot of ways,
because he knew he was big enough and could handle a shovel
and that sort of thing. It's a sort of camaraderie, the banter, the
freedom, being outdoors. Not having to put up with the inhouse
politics, the bollocks, the backstabbing, the typical office mentality. And he does like being outside, enjoys the sun on his back
and stuff like that. Then you get stuck in it, sucked in. You get
used to a certain life-style, and without spending a lot of time
saving the money up, you can't actually get out of it. You need x
amount of money to tread water while you're training to do something else. So you end up getting caught in it. It's a job. You weren't
born with a silver spoon in your mouth so you could just play
around doing whatever you liked whenever you wanted, so then
you've got to do something and this is a worthwhile job.

The other thing Stewart says about his sort of work, it's not
that he doesn't enjoy doing it, because he does (some of the time),
but the working conditions are piss-poor, and we are grossly, grossly
underpaid for a lot of what we do. And under-recognised. And
under-respected.

But as a ganger Stewart still feels something of Peter's determi-
nation to do a job properly, yes. His mate Lee gets annoyed with
him sometimes, he'd want to be a lot more cavalier about it.

Working inheritance   Working with Peter, for a start, it's made us
very useful at work. He's taught us that, when you were actually
working with him as an adult, you use your initiative rather
than stand there and say, What do I do next? And being practi-
cally-minded in approaching problems, how to get around them
or over them. Take a basic thing like lifting something a bit
heavy, if you haven't got anything hydraulic around, you could

use a system of either levers and wedges or a Spanish windlass.

Anything to do with construction and building and the gaswork, and to that degree the waterwork that Stewart has done, has been through the experience we've gained with Peter. It's not so much actually sitting down and teaching us, because we were there to do it. You'd got to learn, and he'd pretty much got the best way of doing it usually, so you pick it up. Over the years of working with him, you came to understand the method, that there was a method to it. He always showed us.

In a sense I suppose it's quite a typical thing, especially a working-class thing, of the knowledge and the trade being handed down from father to son. We started to work with him as kids, and you pick up a little thing or two there, then as you get older you might be doing the odd day with him, and end up working independently, like both of us have done. And it's all through those skills that you learned in those early years. And the same with the sea-going things, inasmuch that we spent x amount of years in the merchant navy and already knew a lot about the sea through Peter, before going to sea. And likewise when Mark has done his exams for the gas qualifications, and also the Road Works Act and so on, that is for the most part what he's picked up and learned from him.

So to a degree we've emulated him, yes. Another important thing we've learned from him is to speak out. We can all hold the floor. And both Stefan and Stewart have tried to emulate a certain type of affection involved in taking the piss out of somebody. If you didn't like them, you wouldn't take the piss out of them, but if you like them, you'll have the crack with them and take the piss.

Fun father Stewart can remember dancing to some good ska reggaes with Pete. That was fun. But it was not something he'd do in front of other people. Because we didn't have the TV we got into books more, and music. There's always been a lot of music in the house, that's why all of us at some stage have been really heavily into music. And we listened to the radio a lot, 'Just a Minute', 'Sorry I haven't a Clue' and 'The Navy Lark'.

Stefan can remember a lot of story-telling going on, and being read to, before you were reading yourself, there was a fair bit of that. There was friends that used to read to us, like Tony B and Antonia.

As a family we've always had a good social life. Lots of people dropping in, lots of very good friends coming to see us, and staying. Including some who would have been at odds with the sort of person Peter was if they saw him at work, the sort of people you wouldn't expect him to mix with. He claimed to be a part-time hippy but Stewart can remember him sitting down and talking to him sometimes and saying, What do you think about those weird people who come round? He wasn't too sure about a lot of them. But then maybe that was because most of them were non-productives.

We did have an awful lot of fun, we had all these adults that were willing to join in and play games, and we could go to adult parties and not feel like we were the token children. In the same way as Peter and Wendy come to our parties now. They enjoy the company of our friends, and if it's an open invite we go en masse, we always have done.

Peter would make us laugh, all the time. He used to play the guitar and make up songs about Wendy and things like that. I mean he couldn't play but he'd just strum chords and sing funny songs. Or just goofing about, like for a couple of days he wouldn't talk, he'd whistle. Drive you barmy.

He's stayed young   It's strange how well our friends get on with Peter, like he always has the wind-up when they first come in, sort of giving them the interrogation. There was one kiddy, Stephen Smith, Peter would ask him in a great deep voice, What's your name boy? And he'd pipe up all nervous, Stephen Smith, sir. But there's friends of Stewart's from years back, now that he's moved out, they still come round. Some of them say they can relate better to Peter and Wendy than they can to their own parents, there's less of a generation gap. It's not that he's immature, but he's stayed young. But also he doesn't talk down to a youngster, he treats them like a human being, he doesn't patronise.

Going out fishing was good. There was bits that we didn't like, like if you got stuck underneath the boat doing the barnacles and things like that, or polishing the engine on that Me Mujer. But the actual fishing side of it we loved.

We used to go out on a lot of day trips. Because we've not been that close to related family members, we've always had a very close group of friends, and especially Stefan can remember, from his

24. Father and sons building the allotment shed in the late 1980s: Mark, Stefan, Peter and Stewart.

first memories in the early seventies, going out in big groups, almost like a coachload of people, going up to Sheffield Park and places like that, and up to the Horniman Museum, one time. There was a lot of that used to go on. And summer holidays, one summer we went down and stayed in Dorset with Chris and Mary. That was quite good fun. Though not without its confrontations, even that.

A lot of love   Thinking about how outsiders would view it, they might term it as physical abuse. But we're still together as a family and as every day passes in some ways we get closer and closer, and that's what doing this book has really rammed home. We've learned about certain things, and certainly more about Peter, and he's been ready to talk.

We've come to understand, as we've got older, that some of the anger was because of the hard times. Peter and Wendy had a very hard time, and they had to be very strong to get themselves, and eventually us, through that. As a kid you don't even understand there's been hard times, but when you think back now you say, Well, if you've got the threat of eviction and things like that hanging over your heads, and all these other stresses, and a couple of kids running around and screaming, who don't understand, and they just keep on and on, then you might fly off the handle. At the time, as a kid, you just think, Well this is a bit outrageous, but looking back at it, it's not surprising. But if Peter had the chance to start again, he would quite possibly do it differently.

It wouldn't be fair to analyse Peter and say, Oh he showed his love with his fists, or any crap like that. When we think back on the relationship we've had with our parents, there's not very much but good there, there's a lot of love. We all get on well, the fact we are quite happy to do all this for the book shows the feelings, the love and the respect we've all got for each other. And the fact that Peter and Wendy were just amateur friends as well, so to speak, so you've got the best of both worlds.

Breaking the cycle   I think Peter will have felt a certain sense of achievement if this book turns into a success. A lot of people would have said, Oh you've just been a man who's done working on the farm, working on the roads, you're just another digit in the world. Whereas he's always wanted to be something and to have a landmark that was left by him.

The book gives him a sense of who he is, what he has been, and a sense of value to that. It's something tangible that carries on after he's not here, for people to know about what life is like, and what his life was like. And he's also said, about the three of us in relation to him, that that's part of what he's done with his life as well.

From things that have come to light regarding writing this book, he didn't have a happy childhood, he was abused. It's become more apparent how he was in his younger days, how that affected him and how he's changed as he's got older. And his not wanting to repeat what happened to him. We've always grown up with a reasonably mature attitude, and obviously with any kids of our own, like Jake, we're not going to sort of automatically follow on. Looking back on it, we know there was a reason, and the cycle has been broken.

INDEX